They Knew How to Pray

Expository Sermons on the
Prayer Lives of Biblical Heroes

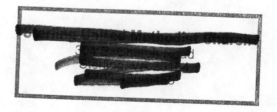

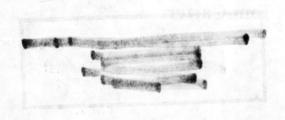

They Knew How to Pray

*Expository Sermons
on the Prayer Lives
of Biblical Heroes*

Tom Carter

BAKER BOOK HOUSE
Grand Rapids, Michigan 49516

Contents

Preface

Picture yourself standing with Moses more than three thousand years ago as he pleaded with God to spare the stiff-necked people of Israel. Try to imagine lifting your hands to heaven with David as he uttered one of his prayerful psalms, lying prostrate with Elijah as he begged the Lord to restore a boy to life, kneeling beside the apostle Paul as he interceded for his spiritual children, or watching the Lord Jesus sweat drops of blood while praying in the Garden of Gethsemane. Because prayer is more caught than taught, I think these experiences would have stamped an indelible impression of God's Spirit on your own prayer life.

Perhaps the next best thing to being there is to study the texts that expose the prayer lives of these and other biblical heroes. Fourteen such studies appear in the following pages, plus a concluding message on Christ's design for the prayer life of today's Christian, as revealed in the most famous prayer ever lifted to heaven—the Lord's Prayer.

I preached these chapters as sermons to my congregation, because I was eager for God's people to develop biblical prayer lives of their own. For years I had been telling them to pray, but I wasn't showing them how. What better models could I hold up to them, I finally thought, than those in the Bible itself? With the exception of Christ, the people discussed in these sermons were not perfect, but they knew how to pray.

I invite you to listen to their cries, feel their spiritual passion, and allow their hearts to mold yours. The lives of the biblical prayer warriors are not historical relics to be admired in the museum of a dead book; they are patterns we should follow in daily life as we are nourished by the living Word of God.

My prayer is that these expository messages will be used for the continuous encouragement of believers.

1

The Prayer Life
of Abraham

Practicing Friendship with God

When Joseph Scriven was a young man, he was deeply in love and engaged to be married. But shortly before the wedding day in 1855, his bride-to-be accidentally drowned. Scriven was plunged into the deepest sorrow, as was his mother. From his home in Canada he wrote and sent this poem to his mother in Ireland to comfort her:

> What a friend we have in Jesus,
> All our sins and griefs to bear!
> What a privilege to carry
> Everything to God in prayer!
> O what peace we often forfeit,
> O what needless pain we bear,
> All because we do not carry
> Everything to God in prayer.

Today this poem has become one of our best-loved hymns. It emphasizes the friendship available to us in Jesus Christ. I think we tend to overlook that. We speak of Christ as our Savior, Lord, master, redeemer, and king. Of course he is all those things. But he wants to be our friend, too. In John 15:15 he told his disciples, "No longer do I call you slaves; . . . but I have called you friends."

The only person ever specifically named friend of God in the Bible is Abraham. Three different passages bestow that title on him: 2 Chronicles 20:7; Isaiah 41:8; James 2:23. There are a number of reasons for Abraham being named friend of God, but I believe the best is his prayer life. It shows us how to practice friendship with God.

Friends of God Pray in Jesus' Name

Three times in the early accounts of Abraham we read that "he built an altar to the LORD and called upon the name of the LORD" (Gen. 12:8; see also Gen. 13:4, 18). An altar, of course, is a place of sacrifice. In the Old Testament, lambs and other animals were placed on an altar and slaughtered as offerings to God. Therefore, Abraham shed the blood of an animal—probably a lamb—when he prayed to the Lord.

The New Testament makes it clear that Jesus is our "Lamb of God who takes away the sin of the world" (John 1:29). All the animal sacrifices in the Old Testament pointed ahead to Christ's sacrifice of himself on Calvary's cross. This is why we pray "in Jesus' name." When we say that, we mean, "Heavenly Father, I have no personal right to approach you. But Jesus has every right, and he is my Savior. So I make these requests in his name—that is, through his merit, for his sake, and for his glory."

That kind of prayer gets results. Jesus' name carries

authority at the Father's throne. Christ alone can open the door into God's presence and give us the right to be heard. That's because he alone makes us presentable to the Father by virtue of his death on the cross for our sins.

Often I've heard people pray to the Father in his own name. But according to 1 Timothy 2:5, we require a mediator, and the only one who will suffice is Jesus. Christ himself promised, "Whatever you ask the Father in My name He will give you" (John 16:23 NKJV).

Abraham was a man on the move. But at his different stopping places he built altars of prayer to God. Commentator Matthew Henry says, "Wherever Abraham had a tent, God had an altar." Do you have an altar in your "tent" —(your home) where everyone comes together for prayer to the heavenly Father through Jesus Christ? A family *altar* can *alter* your family. When I was a child, our family would gather in the living room every evening for Bible reading and prayer. And now I practice that with my wife and children. Believe me, it influences every part of our lives.

In the remainder of this study we will focus our attention on Abraham's great prayer for the wicked city of Sodom, found in Genesis 18. It is the first extended prayer recorded in the Bible.

Friends of God Pray for Others

When Abraham learned that the Lord was about to punish the people of Sodom, he prayed for them. We call this kind of prayer intercession. Abraham might have said, "If the Sodomites are going to be judged, that's their problem, not mine. I have enough needs of my own to pray about; I can't concern myself with the needs of others." But instead, this is how he interceded with God for them: "Suppose there are fifty righteous within the city; wilt Thou indeed sweep it away and not spare the place for the sake of the fifty righteous who are in it?" (Gen. 18:24).

I see three people or groups for whom Abraham was praying. First, he was interceding for his nephew Lot, who lived in Sodom and believed in the Lord (2 Peter 2:7, 8). The patriarch did not want him to perish in the destruction of the city. Second, Abraham was interceding for other righteous people in Sodom who had hearts for God. At this point he felt there were at least forty-nine. And third, this prayer warrior was interceding even for the wicked in Sodom. He begged the Lord to spare them, as well as the believers, from punishment.

These are the same three groups of people for whom we should be interceding: our families, our larger family of Christian brothers and sisters, and a lost world that does not know Jesus.

Do you pray for the salvation and spiritual growth of your family members? If you're a parent, you surely want to see your children become socially well adjusted, earn high grades in school, and be successful in life. You are probably helping them reach these goals and are praying for those results. But are you also asking God to save them from sin and the judgment to come? This is where intercession begins.

The second level reaches beyond our blood line to our spiritual family. Do you pray for your pastor, your church, the missionaries it supports, and other Christians you know? Although already saved from God's wrath, they are still in the thick of spiritual warfare against Satan and his kingdom of darkness. So they need prayer, too.

Finally, do you plead with God for nonbelievers by name? How many of them are you praying for?

These three levels of intercession mark a person as God's

friend. Why? Because the Lord himself is deeply interested in seeing lost people rescued from their sins. He does not want to judge people. The Bible says he "desires all men to be saved and to come to the knowledge of the truth" (1 Tim. 2:4), and that he is "not wishing for any to perish but for all to come to repentance" (2 Peter 3:9). If that's the way you feel about others, you are in agreement with God. And if you put that feeling into practice by praying for non-Christians whom you know, you are God's friend.

The same holds true when you intercede for believers. The longest recorded prayer of Christ in Scripture is dedicated to his disciples (John 17). This was one way he showed them his love.

John Welsh was a Scottish pastor in the late sixteenth century. He often left his bed in the middle of the night, wrapped himself in a warm blanket, and interceded for his people. His wife would beg him to go back to sleep, but he would reply, "I have the souls of three thousand to answer for, and I do not know how it is with many of them." John Welsh knew how to practice friendship with God.

In my own ministry I pray name by name through our church directory of members and friends. As their pastor I feel I owe that to them. And they owe me their prayers, too. Christians have a duty to pray for their spiritual leaders, for people who request their prayers, and for those who don't know Jesus.

Friends of God Pray Compassionately

The biblical record is clear that the city of Sodom was ripe for judgment. In Genesis 19 we learn that homosexuality was a form of recreation to them. We get our word *sodomy* from this story. The sin of these people was so great

that it was about to evoke fire and brimstone out of heaven
(Gen. 19:24).

Yet Abraham had a heart for the Sodomites. Instead of
saying, "It's about time you judged those perverts, Lord,"
he cried out for their salvation. Where did he learn this
compassion? From the heart of God. The patriarch lived
in intimate fellowship with the Lord, his friend, and that's
how he became like him.

Not everyone in the Old Testament shared Abraham's
heart for the lost. Take Jonah. He defied God's order to
preach to the people of Nineveh, because he did not want
them converted. If you had asked him what the Ninevites
were good for, he would have answered, "To fuel the fires
of hell!"

Tragically, compassion for the lost was rare among Jews
in Old Testament times. Because they were God's "chosen"
people, they concluded that other nations were not chosen. But to the contrary, the reason the Lord had chosen
Israel was to take his salvation to the ends of the earth
(Isa. 49:6).

Israel failed to fulfill God's commission. And now Jesus
has entrusted it to us. The church is Plan B on God's
agenda for the world—and there is no Plan C. In Acts 1:8
our Lord handed us the same assignment God had given
Israel in Isaiah 49:6—to carry the good news of salvation
to all the world. Obeying that commission requires compassion. No one who doesn't care about people will seek
to introduce them to Christ.

A man was telling his neighbor how his church had
fired their pastor and hired a better one. "All our former
pastor ever did was tell us we were going to hell," he complained.

"What does the new pastor say?" the neighbor asked.

"The new pastor says we're going to hell, too."

"Then what's the difference?" the neighbor wanted to know.

"Well," the church member said, "when the first pastor said it, he sounded like he was glad of it. But when the new man says it, it sounds like it breaks his heart."

In his book *A Passion for Souls* John Henry Jowett said, "The gospel of a broken heart demands the ministry of a bleeding heart. We can never heal needs that we do not feel."

Are you burdened for the lost, or have you lost your burden? Maybe you pray that certain individuals will come to know Christ. But do you voice their names to the Father merely with your lips, or also with your heart? The Holy Spirit breaks hard hearts by means of soft ones.

Friends of God Pray in Faith

As the story continues, Abraham asked the Lord, "Shall not the Judge of all the earth deal justly?" (Gen. 18:25).

Abraham was saying, "Surely Lord, you will deal justly. Therefore, I'm convinced you will not snuff out the righteous with the wicked in Sodom." He was praying in faith!

Many times my prayers have fallen short right there. I've interceded for non-Christians by name over a period of years, yet they've remained unconverted. And then I've begun wondering if God is really interested in bringing them to Christ. I've found myself praying like this: "Lord, I love this person and desire his salvation enough to plead with you all these years to make him new. But I see no results. Don't you care?"

That's a faithless prayer. God cared enough about me and my friend's salvation to send his only Son to the cross. Jesus cared enough to spill his blood and endure hell for us. I don't know why the Lord doesn't always turn people from their sins as soon as we ask him to. But I invariably come back to this: he is infinitely more concerned about perishing people than we are. That wife who cries her heart out to the Lord day and night for fifty years, pleading for her husband's salvation, has not yearned for him as much as has the heavenly Father. She can have every confidence that God cares far more than she does.

George Müller left a lifelong record of his prayers and the Lord's answers—more than twenty-five thousand of them. When someone asked him to explain his secret, Müller replied, "Have faith in God."

I'm sure Müller laid the stress on those last two words: "faith *in God*." Some people believe that prayer has its own innate power. If that were true, we could babble prayers like parrots, without any understanding, and receive miracles. What gives prayer its power is the Lord to whom we appeal. People all over the world are praying right now to false gods. For all the good it will do them, they may as well be uttering gibberish. Our faith should not be in prayer for its own sake, but in our prayer-answering God.

Friends of God Pray Boldly

Once the Lord promised Abraham that he would spare the whole city of Sodom for the sake of fifty righteous people, the patriarch took a bold step. He asked: "'Suppose the fifty righteous are lacking five, wilt Thou destroy the whole city because of five?' And He said, 'I will not destroy it if I find forty-five there'" (Gen. 18:28).

Most of us would have been satisfied when God agreed to pass over the city for the sake of fifty believers who might be in it. We would have reasoned, "I'd better not push my luck by asking the Lord to suspend his judgment for the sake of forty-five." But Abraham didn't think that way. He was bold in his new request because he was God's friend.

Hebrews 4:16 (NKJV) invites us to "come boldly to the throne of grace." God does not want us to be timid in prayer. The Person we are approaching is our heavenly friend, not some grouchy old scrooge.

Boldness, however, does not rule out reverence. Just before making this request, Abraham compared himself to "dust and ashes" in the Lord's presence (Gen. 18:27). Humility and reverence are always in order when we stand before an infinitely holy God. But still, we can be bold in our requests.

Friends of God Pray Persistently

When the Lord promised a stay of execution for Sodom if forty-five righteous people could be found there, Abraham took that as a go-ahead for continued prayer.

> And he spoke to Him yet again and said, "Suppose forty are found there?" And He said, "I will not do it on account of the forty." Then he said, "Oh may the Lord not be angry, and I shall speak; suppose thirty are found there?" And He said, "I will not do it if I find thirty there." And he said, "Now behold, I have ventured to speak to the Lord; suppose twenty are found there?" And He said, "I will not destroy it on account of the twenty." Then he said, "Oh may the Lord not be angry, and I shall speak only this once; suppose ten are found there?" And He said, "I will not destroy it on account of the ten" (Gen. 18:29–32).

Some people would call this pestering God in prayer. I call it persisting. There's a fine line of difference between the two. We pester God when we continue praying for something he has forbidden, acting like a child who keeps asking for something all day long, after his parents have already said no.

Persistent prayer continues seeking until God gives an answer. Because the Lord kept granting Abraham's requests, our hero kept pleading for the people of Sodom. So, far from merely putting up with Abraham's petitions, God was inviting them by giving *yes* answers one after another. Jesus, too, encouraged us to persist in prayer in his parables of the friend at midnight (Luke 11:5–8) and the importunate widow (Luke 18:1–8).

Some of heaven's blessings fall into our hands like ripe fruit off a tree when we ask the heavenly Father for them. But others will not come down unless we shake the tree again and again. That's where the intensity of persistent prayer comes in. It proves we are serious about receiving God's gifts.

I cannot help but wonder why Abraham didn't continue asking the Lord to spare Sodom all the way down to the sake of one person. Who knows? If he had done that, the city might not have gone up in smoke. But I'm inclined to believe that because Abraham was God's friend, he understood that Sodom's outrageous sin could not go unpunished, except for the sake of at least ten people whose hearts were in tune with the Lord.

Friends of God Pray Successfully

Six times in Genesis 18 Abraham pled for the people of Sodom, and six times he received yes answers on the spot. The Lord did not stop giving until Abraham stopped asking.

What was the secret of his power in prayer? He prayed by means of the proper sacrifice; he prayed according to God's will; he prayed in faith; and his attitude was humble, reverent, bold, and persistent. All these things add up to this simple statement: Abraham's prayer life marks him as the friend of God.

Personal Application

Our great need is to cultivate a deeper friendship with the Lord Jesus Christ. Most of us cannot sincerely sing this verse from Fanny Crosby's hymn "Draw Me Nearer":

> O the pure delight of a single hour
> That before Thy throne I spend,
> When I kneel in prayer, and with Thee, my God,
> I commune as friend with Friend!

If we were honest, our words to that tune would probably sound like this:

> O the pure delight of a single hour
> That before the tube I spend;
> When I kneel to adjust the TV set,
> I come to my best friend.

What we need is a change of best friends. I end this study as I began it, with a verse from Joseph Scriven's great hymn "What a Friend We Have in Jesus":

> Have we trials and temptations?
> Is there trouble anywhere?
> We should never be discouraged;
> Take it to the Lord in prayer!
> Can we find a friend so faithful,
> Who will all our sorrows share?
> Jesus knows our every weakness;
> Take it to the Lord in prayer!

2

The Prayer Life of Moses

*Standing in the Gap
Between God and Man*

One of the great Old Testament types of Jesus Christ is Moses. Numbers 12:3 reports that he was the humblest man on earth; Jesus said, "I am . . . humble in heart" (Matt. 11:29). Moses parted the Red Sea by God's power (Exod. 14:21); Jesus rebuked an angry storm at sea, making the crashing waves become perfectly calm (Mark 4:39). Moses could have had the treasures of Egypt, but he turned them down (Heb. 11:24–26); when Satan tempted Jesus with all the kingdoms of the world, our Lord also said no (Matt. 4:8–10).

Many other parallels between Moses and Christ could be drawn. But perhaps the most striking is found in their prayer lives. Both were known for their intercession with

God on behalf of sinful people. Apart from Christ, Moses is surely the finest example in Scripture of a man who pled with God for the lost. With six wide brush strokes his prayer life paints a portrait of the biblical intercessor.

An Intercessor Pleads Continuously for the Most Hardened and Undeserving People

The classic example of a hardened unbeliever in the Bible is Pharaoh. He was unwilling to let Israel leave Egypt to worship the Lord in the wilderness. So God inflicted him and his people with ten terrifying plagues. Each one was designed to cause Pharaoh to repent, but he continually hardened his heart. On four occasions, however, he did ask Moses to pray for him. The first was during the plague of frogs:

> Pharaoh called for Moses and Aaron and said, "Entreat the LORD that He remove the frogs from me and from my people; and I will let the people go, that they may sacrifice to the LORD.". . . and Moses cried to the LORD concerning the frogs which He had inflicted upon Pharaoh. And the LORD did according to the word of Moses, and the frogs died out. . . . But when Pharaoh saw that there was relief, he hardened his heart and did not listen to them (Exod. 8:8–15).

The plague of insects evoked Pharaoh's second request for prayer. Exodus 8:30–32 tells the result:

> So Moses went out from Pharaoh and made supplication to the LORD. And the LORD did as Moses asked, and removed the swarms of insects from Pharaoh. . . . But Pharaoh hardened his heart this time also, and he did not let the people go.

Most of us would have given up on Pharaoh by then. But when the plague of hail ruined the crops of Egypt, "Pharaoh sent for Moses and Aaron, and said to them, 'I have sinned this time . . . I and my people are the wicked ones. Make supplication to the LORD . . . and I will let you go'" (Exod. 9:27, 28).

Moses saw straight through Pharaoh's hypocrisy and told him, "I know that you do not yet fear the LORD God" (Exod. 9:30).

Yet even that did not prevent Moses from interceding for Pharaoh, as the text goes on to show:

> So Moses went out of the city from Pharaoh, and spread out his hands to the LORD; and the thunder and the hail ceased, and rain no longer poured on the earth. But when Pharaoh saw that the rain and the hail and the thunder had ceased, he sinned again and hardened his heart . . . and he did not let the sons of Israel go (Exod. 9:33–35).

Later, during the plague of locusts:

> Pharaoh hurriedly called for Moses and Aaron, and he said, "I have sinned against the LORD your God and against you. Now therefore, please forgive my sin only this once, and make supplication to the LORD your God, that He would only remove this death from me." And he [Moses] went out from Pharaoh and made supplication to the LORD. So the LORD shifted the wind to a very strong west wind which took up the locusts and drove them into the Red Sea; not one locust was left in all the territory of Egypt. But the LORD hardened Pharaoh's heart, and he did not let the sons of Israel go (Exod. 10:16–20).

This is the fourth time Moses interceded successfully for a man who kept hardening his own heart. In this final passage it says that God hardened the king's heart. Because Pharaoh had repeatedly hardened his own heart, the Lord gave him up to his own depravity. Yet Moses still prayed for him.

Have you ever said about someone, "It's useless to pray for him; he's sold out to sin. He'll never become a Christian." That person might be your own spouse, someone you work with, or a notoriously wordly movie star. If you don't have faith to pray for people like that, then you've failed the first lesson on intercession.

An Intercessor Seeks the Glory of God, Not Personal Glory

In the fourteenth chapter of Numbers, God's people were grumbling against him. They even accused God of leading them to the Promised Land so they could be killed there.

> And the LORD said to Moses, "How long will this people spurn Me? And how long will they not believe in Me, despite all the signs which I have performed in their midst? I will smite them with pestilence and dispossess them, and I will make you into a nation greater and mightier than they" (Num. 14:11, 12).

The people of Israel had been a source of endless heartache to Moses with their murmuring, rebellion, and unbelief. And now they were at his mercy. With one nod of his head, Moses could rid himself of the sons of Israel forever. He could begin raising up a new nation called the sons of Moses. This was his opportunity to become great at the expense of people who had given him nothing but trouble.

But Moses said to the LORD, ". . . Now if Thou dost slay this people as one man, then the nations who have heard of Thy fame will say, 'Because the LORD could not bring this people into the land which He promised them by oath, therefore He slaughtered them in the wilderness.' But now, I pray, let the power of the LORD be great. . . . Pardon, I pray, the iniquity of this people according to the greatness of Thy lovingkindness. . . ." So the LORD said, "I have pardoned them according to your word" (Num. 14:13–20).

Instead of seizing glory for himself, Moses sought glory for his Lord. He knew the people of Israel did not deserve to be forgiven. So he did not base his plea on any goodness in them. He argued that if God should wipe out his people, the other nations would not understand. They would say the Lord was like all the other worldly gods—unable to accomplish his purposes. And that would not reflect well on the divine reputation.

If Moses could figure that out, couldn't God? Of course! He knew it all along. Therefore, he was only testing Moses when he threatened to destroy Israel. Just before Jesus fed five thousand men from one boy's lunch, he asked Philip, "Where are we to buy bread, that these may eat?" But the gospel writer adds, "And this He was saying to test him; for He Himself knew what He was intending to do" (John 6:5, 6). I think God was also testing Moses when he threatened to exterminate Israel and make a great nation of Moses' children. And Moses passed his test. He overcame selfish ambition and pursued glory for God alone.

When you pray for the salvation of a friend, what is your greatest motivation? Love for your friend? A higher spiritual incentive than that is the glory of God. We should yearn for the reign of Jesus to spread to more and more people, that he might take his rightful place as King of kings.

Suppose there should be a scandal in your church. The pastor gets caught embezzling money from the offering collections. In disgust many of the members walk out, and the church's very survival is now threatened. Your heart is deeply wounded, and you begin to pray that the church will bounce back. But why do you pray this way? So that you won't be a laughingstock anymore? That's tempting, isn't it? But our primary concern should be the honor of Christ. We should be grieved for the damage that has come to the reputation of our Lord. True intercessors can pray with the psalmist, "Not to us, O LORD, not to us, but to Thy name give glory" (Ps. 115:1).

An Intercessor Shows a Sacrificial Love for People

One of the darkest days in Israel's history occurred when they constructed a golden calf and worshiped it. Concerning that idolatry, Moses cried out to God:

"Alas, this people has committed a great sin, and they have made a god of gold for themselves. But now, if Thou wilt, forgive their sin—and if not, please blot me out from Thy book which Thou hast written!" (Exod. 32:31, 32).

Moses made no excuses for his people's guilt. He confessed their worship of the golden calf as "a great sin." We may have expected him to say, "Therefore, punish them for it." Instead he cried out for them to be forgiven. And with reckless abandon Moses begged God to blot his name out of the book of life if God refused to forgive Israel.

That's sacrificial love. Every time I read this passage,

I'm convicted of my own lack of it. The apostle Paul shared a kindred spirit with Moses when he said in Romans 9:3, "I could wish that I myself were accursed, separated from Christ for the sake of my brethren, my kinsmen according to the flesh."

When one of the early Christian martyrs was being tortured, his persecutor scoffed, "And what has your Christ ever done for you that you should endure this?"

The believer answered, "He has done this for me, that in the midst of all my pain, I do nothing else but pray for you." He possessed a love that was willing to sacrifice for the sake of his murderer. He was a genuine intercessor.

Jesus once said, "Greater love has no one than this, that one lay down his life for his friends" (John 15:13). Never was Moses' heart more like Christ's than when he was willing to perish for his people. Jesus, however, was more than merely willing to bear the punishment for us. "Christ died for our sins" (1 Cor. 15:3). Still, the muscle of Moses' intercession was fed by his sacrificial love.

Unlike Moses and Paul, we may not be willing to suffer in hell for others. But are we at least ready to sacrifice our convenience, our time, our energy, and our money to see people come to Christ? If not, our claim to be loving rings hollow, and we have much to learn about intercessory prayer.

An Intercessor Is Used by God to Rescue People from Judgment

In the eleventh chapter of Numbers, Israel again set themselves up for divine judgment:

> Now the people became like those who complain of adversity in the hearing of the LORD; and when the LORD

heard it, His anger was kindled, and the fire of the LORD
burned among them and consumed some of the outskirts
of the camp. The people therefore cried out to Moses, and
Moses prayed to the LORD, and the fire died out (Num.
11:1, 2).

There's no mention of what the people were complaining about. Evidently they had nothing better to do than
whine. So God sent fire, perhaps in the form of lightning,
to consume some of them. The fire broke out at the edge
of camp and would have made its way into the center if
Moses had not pled for Israel. Clearly this is a picture of
how God honors intercessory prayer for the salvation of
sinful people.

Psalm 106:23 looks back on events like this and states
that "He (God) said that He would destroy them, had not
Moses His chosen one stood in the breach before Him, to
turn away His wrath from destroying them."

What a picture! The intercessor stands in the gap between a holy God and sinful, rebellious man. And from
that breach he holds back the divine wrath. Can you think
of a higher ministry than that?

Moses was like Jesus when he prayed from the cross,
"Father, forgive them; for they do not know what they are
doing" (Luke 23:34). In answer to that prayer, three thou-
sand Jews were saved less than two months later on the
day of Pentecost (Acts 2:41). When the skull of the first
Christian martyr, Stephen, was being crushed by stones,
he cried out, "Lord, do not hold this sin against them!"
(Acts 7:60). And in answer to that intercessory prayer,
Jesus converted one of Stephen's murderers, the Pharisee
Saul, who became the apostle Paul.

Don't shrug off intercession as an insignificant exercise.
If you and I fail to pray this way, people we know and love

could spend eternity in hell. God has chosen to work through the prayers of his people as a means to accomplish his goal of mankind's salvation.

An Intercessor Has a Shepherd's Heart

Near the end of Moses' life, in one of his final meetings with God, he prayed:

> "May the LORD, the God of the spirits of all flesh, appoint a man over the congregation, who will go out and come in before them, and who will lead them out and bring them in, that the congregation of the LORD may not be like sheep which have no shepherd" (Num. 27:16, 17).

In Scripture, the words *shepherd* and *pastor* are synonymous. Some pastors who leave or retire from their churches become jealous of their successors. If the new pastor fails miserably, the former one is often tempted to rejoice, even though the church may be dying.

But Moses was made of different stuff. When his time came to surrender the leadership of Israel, he interceded with God for a shepherd to guide the people. This shows that Moses himself possessed a shepherd's heart. His saying "that the congregation of the LORD may not be like sheep which have no shepherd," reminds us of Jesus. When he saw "the multitudes, He felt compassion for them, because they were distressed and downcast like sheep without a shepherd" (Matt. 9:36).

A spiritual shepherd cares for individuals. Jesus made that plain in his parable of the shepherd who searched for his one lost sheep while the other ninety-nine were safe in the fold (Luke 15:3–7). Moses was the leader of more than six hundred thousand men, plus women and children

(Num. 26:2, 51). Yet he never lost sight of the individual. From morning until evening he listened to the problems of those who came to him and offered his counsel (Exod. 18:13–15). We can be sure he also prayed for them individually. His shepherd's heart would see to that.

An Intercessor Finds His Prayers Answered in Jesus Christ

Shortly after Moses and his people had left Egypt, this happened:

> They went out three days in the wilderness and found no water. And when they came to Marah, they could not drink the waters of Marah, for they were bitter; therefore it was named Marah. So the people grumbled at Moses, saying, "What shall we drink?" Then he cried out to the LORD, and the LORD showed him a tree; and he threw it into the waters, and the waters became sweet (Exod. 15:22–25).

The Hebrew word for *tree* in this passage is also found in Deuteronomy 21:23. When Paul quotes this verse in Galatians 3:13, he says it points to the cross. That gives us a clue to the interpretation of this story in Moses' life. The tree that made the bitter waters sweet is a picture of Jesus' cross. It alone sweetens our bitter waters of trials, persecution, and suffering.

God showed Moses the tree in answer to his prayer for his people. This illustrates how Christ crucified is the solution to our intercessory cries for unbelievers. The heavenly Father wants us to realize that nothing less than the blood of his Son, shed at Calvary, can solve man's greatest problem.

Another example of this principle is found in the twenty-first chapter of Numbers:

> And the people spoke against God and Moses, "Why have you brought us up out of Egypt to die in the wilderness? For there is no food and no water, and we loathe this miserable food." And the LORD sent fiery serpents among the people and they bit the people, so that many people of Israel died. So the people came to Moses and said, "We have sinned, because we have spoken against the LORD and you; intercede with the LORD, that He may remove the serpents from us." And Moses interceded for the people (Num. 21:5–7).

Just one cry from the rebels—"Intercede for us"—and Moses fell to his knees. Quickly the answer came from heaven:

> The LORD said to Moses, "Make a fiery serpent, and set it on a standard; and it shall come about, that everyone who is bitten, when he looks at it, he shall live." And Moses made a bronze serpent and set it on the standard; and it came about, that if a serpent bit any man, when he looked to the bronze serpent, he lived (Num. 21:8, 9).

Our Lord Jesus saw in that bronze serpent an illustration of himself dying on the cross. In John 3:14, 15 he said, "And as Moses lifted up the serpent in the wilderness, even so must the Son of Man be lifted up; that whoever believes may in Him have eternal life."

Just as that bronze serpent was the answer to Moses' prayer for his suffering people, the dying Savior is the solution to man's greatest need today. If our prayers for others can be answered with anything less than the blood of Christ, we are not praying deeply enough.

Personal Application

If it were not for someone else's intercessory prayers, would you and I belong to Christ today? Perhaps if we could see this from God's viewpoint, it would be like a vast chain made up of single hooks. Someone hooked onto you through prayer, and you were converted to Christ. Before that, someone else interceded for them, thus forming a previous link. And so it has continued since the early days of Christianity.

Many of these people have brought more than one person to the Savior this way. For them, the links become a network branching out. Some would call this a network of evangelism, and it is. But it begins as a network of intercessory prayer. Right now you and I are at the end of that network. It started two thousand years ago with Jesus Christ, and the line has been unbroken all the way to us.

Now it's our turn to continue the chain and the network. Will these links stop with us? When others have been faithful for so long, will we now be faithless? Today you and I stand in the gap between God and man. But we must do more than just stand there. We must fall on our knees as well.

3

The Prayer Life of Joshua
Three Steps Forward, Two Steps Back

Charles Swindoll has written a book titled *Three Steps Forward, Two Steps Back*. It's filled with advice on how to persevere through pressures like stress, loneliness, temptation, fear, and anger.

I think his title is also a good description of the average Christian's prayer life. Let's face it. We don't chalk up sensational answers to prayer every week. At least I don't. The heavenly Father gives us a few answers to keep us from growing discouraged. But sometimes his answers mystify us. And often we make selfish requests of God or fail to pray for specific needs. Sometimes our prayer lives are more like *one* step forward and *four* back.

You may be surprised to hear that Joshua's prayer life

was inconsistent. In response to his request, the Lord stopped the rotation of the earth so that the Israelites had daylight for an extra day. It was one of the most amazing wonders in all the Bible. But on other occasions Joshua failed miserably in prayer. The book about his life contains four examples from his prayer life. Let's look at them one at a time.

He Surrendered in Prayer

The first account of Joshua in conversation with the Lord is found in Joshua 5. It takes place shortly before the famous battle of Jericho.

> Now it came about when Joshua was by Jericho, that he lifted up his eyes and looked, and behold, a man was standing opposite him with his sword drawn in his hand, and Joshua went to him and said to him, "Are you for us or for our adversaries?" (5:13).

Joshua did not realize it yet, but this man was God. In the next verse he would identify himself as "captain of the host of the LORD," and Joshua would worship him. I believe this "man" was Jesus Christ in preincarnate form.

Since the Lord had a drawn sword in his hand, Joshua asked, "Are you for us or for our adversaries?" He wanted to know if this warrior were going to fight for Israel or for Jericho in the upcoming battle. The answer he received startled him: "And he said, 'No, rather I indeed come now as captain of the host of the LORD'" (5:14).

God was saying, "I'm neither your ally nor your enemy, Joshua. I'm your commander. I haven't come to take sides; I've come to take over. You are hereby dismissed from your post."

What a challenge for Joshua! There are six hundred

thousand soldiers back in the camp, plus women and children, (cf. Num. 26:51) who considered him their commander in chief. He could not resign now, on the eve of the most important battle of his life, could he? Yes, he could. "And Joshua fell on his face to the earth, and bowed down, and said to him, 'What has my lord to say to his servant?'" (5:14).

This great military general was about to break the news to the multitudes of Israel that he was now a buck private under the command of the Lord God. All his plans for capturing the city of Jericho were cancelled. There would be no troops climbing over the wall, no breaking down the gate with a battering ram. All the swords, bows, and arrows were to be put away. Joshua was going to let the Lord call the shots. Recently his mind had been flooded with thoughts of the enemy surrendering to him. But now he surrendered to God.

Joshua's question, "What has my lord to say to his servant?" sounds like the one Paul asked on the day of his conversion: "What shall I do, Lord?" (Acts 22:10). Have you ever said that to Christ? Often we turn that around and say, "Lord, here's what I want you to do for me." Without so much as consulting his will, much less submitting to it, we tell God our plans and try to bribe him into bringing them to pass for us. Or we threaten him that if he does not help us, he will have one less disciple on his list. But this is the opposite of surrendering to Christ as Lord.

At age fifteen I landed a part-time job as night janitor at Overseas Crusades in Palo Alto, California. I mopped the floors, dusted, vacuumed, swept, and generally cleaned when the office was closed. My favorite part was sitting in Luis Palau's chair behind his desk. He was and still is considered the Billy Graham of South America.

One night there was a note waiting for me from Norm Cummings, the president. He wanted to see me the next day. I felt like Belshazzar when he saw the handwriting on the wall. The next afternoon Mr. Cummings let me know that I was dismissed. Fired. Someone else had been given my job. I never felt so ashamed in all my life. What would I tell my parents? How would I explain to my friends? No more sitting in Luis Palau's chair! It was one of the most humbling experiences in my life.

But through it all I learned a spiritual parallel to the lesson God had taught Joshua: To have Christ as Lord means I am fired, and he takes over.

One of our popular Christian hymns is titled "I Surrender All." I suppose you've sung it many times, but have you really yielded your life to Christ? Does his sacrificing love dominate your marriage relationship? Does he control your finances? Is he in command of your work schedule, your hobbies, your recreation, your reading material, and the television and movies you watch? Joshua made a total surrender of himself to the Lord in prayer. That was one quantum leap forward for him. And as you know, the Lord soon gave him a great victory over the city of Jericho when its walls came tumbling down.

He Struggled with Prayer

In the battle of Jericho, the Lord had commanded his people not to take for themselves the spoils after the victory. The plunder was to be reserved completely for God. But a man named Achan defied the divine command. He snatched up a coat, some silver, and a bar of gold, then hid them in his tent. It was his secret sin, but the Lord saw it. As a result, God refused to give Israel the victory in its next campaign against Ai. Israel, overly confident, went down in miserable defeat.

Immediately after the fiasco, before he knew about Achan's sin, Joshua went to the Lord in prayer saying, "Alas, O LORD God, why didst Thou ever bring this people over the Jordan, only to deliver us into the hand of the Amorites, to destroy us?" (Josh.7:7).

Joshua was blaming God for Israel's problems, accusing the Lord of leading them into the Promised Land so their enemies could destroy them. That was the last thing on God's mind. It was not his will for Israel to lose the battle at Ai or anywhere else. Joshua brought his hurts to God, which is commendable, but he was also irreverent and judgmental toward God. He was struggling with prayer.

Joshua went on to say, "If only we had been willing to dwell beyond the Jordan!" (7:7).

Nearly forty years earlier, Joshua had been one of twelve men who spied out the land of Canaan. Ten of them reported to the people, "There are giants in the land, and we can never live there!" But Joshua and Caleb encouraged Israel to trust God to fulfill his promise of giving them the land. Now, however, Joshua sounded like one of the ten spies. It was as though he said, "I wish I had never come into this new country. I wish I had never obeyed you, Lord, by allowing you to guide me here."

Joshua had lived in three different places—Egypt, the wilderness, and Canaan. Each represents an area in our own lives. Israel's slavery to Pharaoh in Egypt symbolizes our slavery to Satan and sin before we met Christ. But God set the people of Israel free and started leading them toward Canaan. That's a picture of our conversion, when we were delivered from the power of sin and Satan and were led into a life of trusting God. But before the Jews reached Canaan, they had to pass through the wilderness. It only takes eleven days to walk across it (Deut. 1:2). But due to Israel's sin, they wandered there forty years. Israel in the wilderness represents the believer who refuses to grow in Christ. We call such people carnal Christians. When they could be enjoying the fulfilling experience of trusting in God's promises, they are content to eke out an existence in the wilderness of doubt, worry, fear, and frustration.

Therefore, when Joshua prayed, "If only we had been willing to dwell beyond the Jordan [in the wilderness]!" he was being carnal. He was unwilling to trust God.

His prayer continues with these words:

> "Oh Lord, what can I say since Israel has turned their back before their enemies? For the Canaanites and all the inhabitants of the land will hear of it, and they will surround us and cut off our name from the earth. And what wilt Thou do for Thy great name?" (Josh. 7:8, 9).

Joshua was dwelling mostly on his own feelings. Granted, he did ask God to protect the reputation of God's name. But first our friend expressed his worry that Israel's name would become a laughingstock.

We imitate Joshua when we nurse bitterness against our heavenly Father for trials he allows us to pass through. Maybe someone in your family died of a painful, lingering illness, such as cancer. You watched the person suffer for over a year and then die in the prime of life. You cried out to God for answers. But when none came, you resented him for what happened. Perhaps you're still carrying anger in your heart toward the Lord after many years. In situations like that, we need to remember that there is always more to life than we can see. God has his reasons that we know nothing about.

In Joshua's case, the Lord went on to explain what his reasons were. He rebuked Israel's leader with these words: "Rise up! Why is it that you have fallen on your face? Israel has sinned . . . they have even taken some of the things under the ban and have both stolen and deceived" (7:10, 11).

God interrupted Joshua's prayer to say, in effect, "Don't blame me for the defeat at Ai. It's Israel's fault." He then gave him instructions for discovering the individual culprit, Achan.

Often in our situations the Lord does not explain the reasons for our troubles. That's where faith comes in. In his moment of weakness Joshua had failed to trust his Lord. And it set him a giant step back in his spiritual walk.

He Skipped over Prayer

The third account of Joshua's prayer life is found in chapter 9. Achan's sin that caused the defeat at Ai had been dealt with, and Israel had claimed its second victory. The citizens of Gibeon heard about Israel's military might and were terrified. So they devised a plan to deceive Joshua into thinking they were from a distant land and posing no threat to him and the nation of Israel. In this way they hoped Joshua would sign a peace treaty with them. Then he would be morally unable to exterminate them, even if their lie were detected.

The plan worked like a charm. The Gibeonites brought worn-out sacks, wineskins, sandals, and clothes to give the impression they had traveled from a distant country. They rescued stale bread out of their garbage heaps and passed it off as bread that had been fresh when they left home. It all looked so convincing.

When they met Joshua, they called themselves his servants three times. Their flattery got them everywhere. Joshua and his assistants took the bait and fell into the devil's trap. "So the men of Israel took some of their provisions, and did not ask for the counsel of the LORD" (9:14).

Joshua thought this was an open-and-shut case, one that required no prayer. But his presumption led to an irreversible mistake that cost Israel dearly for centuries to come. Joshua and his people later had to take time out to fight Gibeon's enemies for them. But more than that, God had set his people apart as a holy nation. Yet they were forced to live with the people of Gibeon, whose background did not nurture their spiritual life.

Today many Christian young persons repeat Joshua's error of failing to seek God's will, such as in their choice of a marriage partner. Like Joshua, they rely on sight. They see someone attractive, fall in love, and get married—without first consulting the Lord. If they would ask for his counsel, they would hear him say that a woman "is free to marry anyone she wishes, but he must belong to the Lord" (1 Cor. 7:39 NIV) and "Do not be bound together with unbelievers" (2 Cor. 6:14). But because they impulsively rush into marriage they force themselves to live in the spiritual distress that makes the Christian life tedious and fruitless.

Perhaps our worst problem in prayer is not that we do it poorly, with mixed motives, or in the wrong words, but that often we don't pray. Cameron Thompson once said, "Heaven must be full of answers to prayer for which no one ever bothered to ask." The French churchman Fenelon said, "Of all the duties commanded by Christianity, none is more essential and yet more neglected than prayer." And John Bunyan wrote, "Prayer will make a Christian stop sinning, or sin will make a Christian stop praying."

Joshua violated the principle that was later expressed in Proverbs 3:5, 6 (NKJV):

> Trust in the LORD with all your heart,
> And do not lean on your own understanding;
> In all your ways acknowledge Him,
> And He shall direct your paths.

Joshua proves that even giants of the faith are prone to make irreversible mistakes when they fail to pray about small matters. He shows us that neglecting to pray makes us insensitive to sin. If he had sought guidance from God, he would have learned that the Gibeonites were lying to him. But because he trusted in his own judgment, he was blind to their sin. Our lack of prayer makes us blind not only to other people's sins but especially to our own. It always results in a step back in our walk with Christ.

He Succeeded through Prayer

In the tenth chapter of Joshua we have the last account of this man in prayer. And it concludes on a happy note. He was engaged in a battle against the Amorites. The day was wearing long, and the job was not finished. Joshua feared that if the sun set, many of his enemies would get away.

Then Joshua spoke to the LORD . . . and he said in the sight of Israel,

> "O sun, stand still at Gibeon,
> And O moon in the valley of Aijalon."
> So the sun stood still and the moon stopped,
> Until the nation avenged themselves of their enemies.

Is it not written in the book of Jashar? And the sun stopped in the middle of the sky, and did not hasten to go down for

about a whole day. And there was no day like that before it
or after it, when the LORD listened to the voice of a man; for
the LORD fought for Israel (Josh. 10:12–14).

What a daring request! Of course we know that the sun
is already still; it doesn't move. But the Bible is speaking in
common, everyday terms. The Lord prolonged the daytime
so that Joshua could complete the victory over his enemies. We might say that Joshua wanted to beat the day-
lights out of the Amorites, and God granted his request.
Verse 14 in the Living Bible reads, "The Lord stopped the
sun and moon—all because of the prayer of one man."

Like Joshua, you and I are engaged in a warfare. Ours is
a spiritual one. Some Christians are unaware of this, but
that does not change anything. Ephesians 6:12 says, "For
our struggle is not against flesh and blood [human
beings], but against the rulers, against the powers, against
the worldforces of this darkness, against the spiritual
forces of wickedness in the heavenly places."

Note that word *struggle*. We struggle against Satan and
his kingdom. We struggle for people who are in his grasp.
But our human willpower, resolutions, and good inten-
tions to fight this battle will always be insufficient. On our
own we are no match for the devil. Nothing less than the
power of God can bring us the victory. And that's where
prayer comes in.

The passage on spiritual warfare goes on to say, "With
all prayer and petition pray at all times in the Spirit, and
with this in view, be on the alert with all perseverance and
petition for all the saints" (Eph. 6:18). Notice that this one
verse speaks of prayer four times.

Do you live with a warfare mentality? Some believers
don't know they are in a battle, while others know it but
don't appeal to the Holy Spirit in prayer for help.

Joshua teaches us that God is willing to grant colossal prayer requests to aid us in spiritual warfare. So don't think that you will never be able to conquer your besetting sin. Surely it is too strong for you, but you have a Lord in heaven who is willing to make the sun stand still, if necessary, to give you the victory. When this promise sinks in and you start claiming it in prayer, then like Joshua you will take a great step forward in your relationship with God.

Personal Application

As we look back on the four examples from Joshua's prayer life, the main lesson I want you to see is that weaknesses, mistakes, and failures in prayer should not discourage us. Too many Christians give up on prayer completely, for all practical purposes, because they know they are not perfect at it. Let's understand that even Joshua —who stopped the earth on its twenty-four-hour rotation through one of his prayers—was often a klutz at it.

The important thing is to keep moving with Christ. Sometimes you will take a spill and disappoint yourself as well as Jesus. But if you can look back over a year and see that you've taken two steps back but three forward, you will find that you have grown. And when God gets through with growing Christians, they become Christ-like.

4

The Prayer Life of Gideon
Asking God for Signs

Kathy and Marty were Christian friends of mine in college. Although they hardly knew each other, Kathy had a huge crush on Marty. So she told the Lord in prayer, "If Marty asks me out on a date, let that be your sign that he's the one I'm going to marry."

A week or two later, Marty phoned Kathy and asked her out. She gladly accepted. But after about two dates, Marty realized he wasn't interested in Kathy, and the dating part of the relationship was off. Kathy was not only heartsick but bewildered. Hadn't God given her the sign she had begged him for? Why, then, was there no future in the relationship? Had the heavenly Father failed to keep his promise?

I think the Lord was telling Kathy, "I'm not going to

allow you to manipulate me." She was trying to make God
follow her lead, when it should have been the other way
around.

In Matthew 12:39 Jesus said, "An evil and adulterous
generation craves for a sign; and yet no sign shall be given
to it but the sign of Jonah the prophet." That makes sense.
After all, Hebrews 11:6 teaches that faith is what pleases
God. But in the sixth chapter of the Book of Judges, a man
named Gideon asked the Lord for three signs, and all
three of them were granted. These are Gideon's only
prayer requests recorded in Scripture.

Gideon wasn't the only one in the Bible, by the way,
who prayed for signs. In Genesis 24 Abraham sent his servant to the city of Nahor to find a wife for his son, Isaac.
When the servant rested at a well, he prayed for a sign. He
told God he would ask the young women for a drink.
Then he requested that the one God had picked out as
Isaac's wife would reply, "And I will water your camels
also." That is how the servant identified Rebekah, for she
responded in those exact words. A brief time later she
married Isaac.

When King Saul's son Jonathan was about to attack the
Philistines, he explained to his armor bearer that he had
asked for a sign from the Lord. They would show themselves to the Philistines, who were at the top of a hill. If
the enemy said, "Stay where you are!" that would be their
signal that God was not going to help them. But if they
said, "Come up here and fight us!" that would be the sign
that the Lord would give them the victory. God honored
the request by showing Jonathan and his armor bearer the
favorable sign, then allowing them to slaughter the
Philistines that day (1 Sam. 14:6–14).

When David feared that Saul was bent on killing him,

Jonathan thought he had nothing to worry about. So the two friends agreed on a sign. David would make himself absent from the dinner table. If Saul thought nothing of it, that would mean he wasn't angry. But if the king flew into a rage, they would take that as confirmation from God that Saul was indeed thirsting for David's blood. Sure enough, Saul revealed his colors by raging when he heard the news of David's absence (1 Sam. 20).

The Old Testament practice of casting lots was another use of signs. It was similar to our flipping a coin. If the lot landed one way, it meant one thing. If it landed another way, it meant something else. This was how the people of Israel inquired into God's will, and the Lord responded to it. (To our minds, the word *lot* sounds uncomfortably close to *lottery*.)

All these examples cause us to ask, "Are we supposed to pray for signs or not? Is it right, or isn't it?" In an attempt to answer that question, we will study the prayer life of Gideon. Let's take a close look at his three prayer requests for signs, all of which were granted.

The Sign of the Fire

The first account of Gideon in prayer begins in Judges 6:12: "And the angel of the LORD appeared to him and said to him, 'The LORD is with you, O valiant warrior.'"

Gideon did not know it yet, but this angel was actually God. In verses 14,16, and 23 he is called the LORD. So while Gideon talked to him, he was actually praying. His first response to the news that God was with him was to doubt:

> Then Gideon said to him, "Oh my lord, if the LORD is with us, why then has all this happened to us? And where

are all His miracles which our fathers told us about, saying, 'Did not the LORD bring us up from Egypt?' But now
the LORD has abandoned us and given us into the hand of
Midian" (v. 13).

At least Gideon was honest with God. He did not try to
hide his doubts, sorrows, and troubles. He explained that
he had serious trouble believing the promise that the Lord
was with him, because he had not seen any evidence of it.
The Midianites had been oppressing Israel. The miracles
performed through Moses and Joshua had ceased. And
instead of having God with Israel, it seemed to our friend
that God had abandoned them.

And the LORD looked at him and said, "Go in this your
strength and deliver Israel from the hand of Midian. Have
I not sent you?" (v. 14).

Here was Gideon's great commission. Yet he protested
that he was too young and insignificant for such a huge
task. "But the LORD said to him, 'Surely I will be with you,
and you shall defeat Midian as one man'" (v. 16).

What a promise! David Livingstone, the great missionary to Africa, wrote in his journal on January 14, 1856:
"Felt much turmoil of spirit today. But I read that Jesus
said, 'Lo, I am with you always,' so there is an end of it!"
A few years later, when he was receiving an honorary doc-
toral degree at the University of Glasgow in Scotland,
Livingstone testified to the assembly concerning that
promise in Matthew 28:20, "On those words I staked
everything, and they never failed."

Gideon had a similar promise from God: "Surely I will
be with you." But his faith was no match for David Livingstone's. He wanted to believe the Lord, but at the moment
he felt he couldn't. "So Gideon said to Him, 'If now I have

found favor in Thy sight, then show me a sign that it is Thou who speakest with me'" (v. 17).

If I had been God I would have denied his request. I would have said, "You have my word on it, Gideon; that's all you need. Trust me." But amazingly, the Lord did it Gideon's way! He waited while Gideon prepared a meal of meat and bread. When it arrived, he told Gideon to place it on a rock in front of him. After that God performed the sign:

> Then the angel of the LORD put out the end of the staff that was in his hand and touched the meat and the unleavened bread; and fire sprang up from the rock and consumed the meat and the unleavened bread. Then the angel of the LORD vanished from his sight (v. 21).

When fire sprang up from a rock and consumed the food, it was a sign to Gideon that the Lord would also consume the Midianites through him. For the moment, at least, he was convinced. He showed his appreciation by building an altar and worshiping the Lord (v. 24).

The Sign of the Fleece

The story continues. The Midianites and Amalekites advanced against Israel. The battle was imminent, and once again God's chosen leader balked in his faith.

> Then Gideon said to God, "If Thou wilt deliver Israel through me, as Thou hast spoken, behold, I will put a fleece of wool on the threshing floor. If there is dew on the fleece only, and it is dry on all the ground, then I will know that Thou wilt deliver Israel through me, as Thou hast spoken." And it was so. When he arose early the next morning and squeezed the fleece, he drained the dew from the fleece, a bowl full of water (vv. 36–38).

It is possible that Gideon regularly slept with a sheep-skin over him, and that every morning both it and the ground were covered with dew. Now he asked God to make only the fleece wet. And sure enough, the Lord performed the miracle. But again we are left with the nagging question, Is Gideon's practice of asking for signs something we can do today?

In her book *The Tapestry* Edith Schaeffer tells of an experience her famous husband, Francis, had when he was nineteen. It was 5:30 A.M. the day he was to leave for college to prepare for the ministry. But when he came downstairs, his father said, "I don't want a son who is a minister, and I don't want you to go." His father dreamed of him becoming a mechanical engineer.

Francis broke the awkward silence by asking to retreat to the cellar to pray. There he tearfully begged God for wisdom. Desperate to know the divine will, he took a coin from his pocket and said, "Heads, I'll go in spite of Dad." When he flipped the coin, it came up heads. Still crying, he pleaded, "God, be patient with me. If it comes up tails this time, I'll go." He tossed the coin again, and it was tails. But he was still unsure of himself. "Once more, God. I don't want to make a mistake with Dad upstairs. Please, now let it be heads again." When the coin landed heads, he was reassured. Francis reappeared from the cellar and told his father he had to go.

Francis Schaeffer went on to become one of the most fruitful Christian leaders of the twentieth century. It would seem, therefore, that he was not out of line to flip his coin those three times. And yet in later years he warned others against seeking to discover God's will that way. He looked back on that experience as something the heavenly Father graciously used, but which he was presumptuous to ask for.

This is how I view Gideon's requests for signs. God did

not owe them to Gideon, but in kindness he worked through them.

Daniel Fuller, in *Give the Winds a Mighty Voice,* tells this story of his father. In 1954 Charles E. Fuller, founder of Fuller Theological Seminary in Pasadena, California, urged his friend Harold Ockenga to become its new president. At the time Ockenga was pastor of the thriving Park Street Church in Boston, and he felt pulled in both directions. He sensed that God might be calling him to Fuller Seminary, but he did not want to give up his regular preaching.

So he laid out a "fleece." Then he put it to the test by flying to Pasadena. There he was a guest in the Fuller home. Throughout the night his host, Charles, had difficulty sleeping. Early in the morning he knocked on Harold's door. Going in, he said, "Harold, I've come to a decision. I want you to take over the Old Fashioned Revival Hour" (the national radio program Fuller preached on every week). Fuller was sixty–seven years old and felt it was time to pass the baton, and he wanted Ockenga to take it.

Hearing that, Harold covered his face with his hands and gasped, "Oh, Charles, that's the fleece! I told the Lord that if the door would be opened for me to carry on my preaching ministry by being on the Old Fashioned Revival Hour, I would take that as an indication that I should move to California and become the president of Fuller Seminary."

The faculty and seminary board were elated to hear the news. Ockenga returned to Boston and announced his resignation from the Park Street Church. But the congregation was deeply grieved. They even organized a caravan of cars to drive to New Hampshire where he was vacationing to show him how much they wanted him to stay. He was deeply touched by their love and began to have second thoughts about his decision.

After much prayer, Ockenga came to the decision that God wanted him to stay in Boston. The "fleece" had not been a final indication of the divine will. With a sense of embarrassment and humility, he asked his church to let him change his mind. They were thrilled to have him do that. Then he also informed the seminary that he had made a mistake.

Harold Ockenga continued as pastor of Park Street Church for another fifteen years, during which time its ministry and world missions continued to grow. And God gave Charles Fuller the health and strength to continue preaching on his national radio program for another thirteen years. Those events seem to confirm the wisdom of Ockenga's changed mind.

These examples from Francis Schaeffer and Harold Ockenga illustrate that laying out a "fleece" is a dangerous thing. I think it was risky even for Gideon, although God condescended to his method. In our age it's especially hazardous, because we possess the full revelation of God's Word.

The Sign of the Floor

After getting his two signs of the fire and the fleece, Gideon still had trouble believing.

> Gideon said to God, "Do not let Thine anger burn against me that I may speak once more; please let me make a test once more with the fleece, let it now be dry only on the fleece, and let there be dew on all the ground." And God did so that night; for it was dry only on the fleece, and the dew was on all the ground (vv. 39, 40).

I think Gideon felt he had been hasty to ask for the dew to stay on the fleece rather than the threshing floor. Wool would naturally hold water longer and in greater amounts than ground. And so to make doubly sure of God's promise, he turned his request around. If God would only make the threshing floor wet and the fleece dry, that would be a genuine miracle.

The next morning it was so. Maybe the Lord was saying to Gideon, "You are the fleece, and all Israel is the floor. The dew of my blessing is going to pour out on you both." In any case, God was being gracious to grant this prayer request. In verse 39 Gideon admitted he was making another "test" of the Lord. He should have known that God's law said, "You shall not put the LORD your God to the test" (Deut. 6:16). His faith was weak, but at least he was eager to become strong. He was like the man who told Jesus, "I do believe; help me in my unbelief" (Mark 9:24).

My mother is a popular Bible teacher at women's conferences. Once she received a phone call from a woman I'll call Susan, who asked her to speak at an upcoming retreat. My mother asked for some time in which to pray about it. Yet she still could not discern a call from God to go. But she did not want to make a decision based only on her feelings, either.

As a last resort after much prayer and still no sense of guidance, she asked God for a sign. She said, "Lord, if they really need me, I don't want to turn them down. So when Susan calls me back, if you want me to speak at that retreat, make her tell me, 'Helen, we need you.' If she uses that word *need*, then I'll know it's your will for me to go, and I'll obey."

A day or two later Susan called again, asking for an

answer. My mother told her, "I can't honestly say I know the Lord wants me to accept your invitation."

To that Susan replied, "Helen, this is more than an invitation. We don't just *want* you to be our speaker; we *need* you!"

When my mother heard that, a joyful smile lit up her face. She immediately informed Susan about her dilemma and the sign she had requested from God. Then she accepted the offer, spoke at the conference, and saw the Lord work in the lives of many women.

Personal Application

Should we then pray for signs? At best, I think it should be used rarely, only after much prayer, searching of Scripture, waiting on the Lord, and only as a last resort. And even then, we have no guarantee that God will respond to it.

A man once challenged me, "If God exists, why doesn't he prove it to me in some visible or audible way?" Later I heard a recording of a demon-possessed woman who was calling in to Bob Larson's Christian radio show, "Talk Back." Listening to the demon in that woman was a fearful reminder of spiritual warfare, to say the least. The demon even acknowledged Christ, just as demons did in the Gospels. I played a cassette tape of that radio program to my friend. It was a convincing sign. But he still would not believe.

The Jews of Jesus' day who were craving for signs were like that. They witnessed dozens of Jesus' miracles, yet they still crucified him. And he gave them yet another sign by rising from the dead. But even then they refused to believe.

Gideon, however, was willing to obey God's will once

he was certain it was the divine will. After Gideon got his signs, God got his man, for in the very next chapter of Judges Gideon led Israel in victory over the Midianites.

Remember also that we are not living in Gideon's age. In his time only the first six books of the Bible had been written, and possibly the Book of Job. But even those books, handwritten on scrolls, were not available to the people to read themselves.

If we want signs, there are two prominent ones we can claim. One is Scripture itself. It speaks to us. It reveals God's will for us. When our faith is in Christ, it assures us of our salvation. And it guides us in our daily decisions.

The other sign is a changed life. Do you have that? Can people see a radical difference Christ has made in you? Are you a new creation? Jesus said, "You will know them by their fruits" (Matt. 7:16, 20). If the Holy Spirit is producing in your life his fruits of "love, joy, peace, patience, kindness, goodness, faithfulness, gentleness, self-control" (Gal. 5:22, 23), you have the unmistakable sign that you belong to Christ and are being used by him. A changed life speaks for itself.

Gideon had a changed life. In the sixth chapter of Judges he was obviously a man of weak faith. His need for signs proved that. But later he became a spiritual giant. In Hebrews 11 we find God's honor roll of Old Testament heroes of faith: Noah, Abraham, Joseph, Moses, Joshua, Samuel, and David. And Gideon is there, too. In Hebrews 11:32 the author writes, "And what more shall I say? For time will fail me if I tell of Gideon" and others.

Is your faith weak? Does it crave signs and tangible evidences? Don't despair. God can build even you into a hero of faith, just as he did Gideon. Just make sure you respond positively to any signs the Lord might be giving you.

Perhaps some you're not even asking for, but they may come in an answer to prayer, a verse of Scripture that pinpoints a problem you have, or a Christian friend who shows a caring heart in your hour of need.

Should we pray for signs? We don't have to. God has already given us many, if we will only have eyes to see them.

5

The Prayer Life of Hannah

Turning Bitterness into Blessing

A missionary family serving in Pakistan returned to the United States for a furlough. Soon a teenage gang attacked their young son and beat him across the face with a nail-studded rope. The boy was blinded in one eye and left with only 10 percent vision in the other. The gang members were caught, tried, and convicted by the court. Throughout the trial, the parents of the injured boy refused to indulge in bitterness. Instead, they expressed to the offenders a willingness to forgive. The mother was quoted in the newspaper as saying, "If necessary, we can live with a physical handicap. But we can't live with bitterness."

Those last words, "We can't live with bitterness," are

true of us all, whether or not we realize it. If we harbor this weed in our hearts, it will choke the flower of joy. Hannah, the mother of Samuel, was deeply pricked by bitterness. First Samuel 1:6 says she was provoked bitterly. And the end of verse 10 reports that she wept bitterly. But soon she was overflowing with joy. Hannah's prayer life, by which God turned her bitterness into blessing, is summed up in three words: trials, trust, and thanksgiving.

Trials Activated Her Prayers

The First Book of Samuel, chapter 1 introduces us to a man, Elkanah, and his two wives, Hannah and Peninnah. Peninnah had many sons and daughters, but as for Hannah, "The LORD had closed her womb. Her rival, however, would provoke her bitterly to irritate her, because the LORD had closed her womb" (1 Sam. 1:5, 6).

Hannah's trial was that she had no children. Your problem might be just the opposite—that you *have* children. At times you'd be willing to say, "Here, Hannah, you can take my kids!"

But this was no laughing matter to Hannah. She believed what Solomon later wrote in Psalm 127:3, 5:

Behold, children are a gift of the LORD;
The fruit of the womb is a reward.
How blessed is the man whose quiver is full of them.

And yet Hannah had none. Mark the repetition of the clause, "the LORD had closed her womb" at the end of verse 6. We are left wondering, Why did God do this? Had Hannah committed some secret sin? Had she recently been rebelling against the Lord? The text does not say. But I think it's safe to conclude that God was not punishing Hannah. The author portrays her as a godly and virtuous woman. No sin of hers is mentioned in this or any other passage.

Why, then, did the Lord close her womb? I believe he wanted to bring Hannah to the point of total dependence on him. God was teaching this woman that he was her only hope of motherhood. If her greatest goal in life was ever going to be fulfilled, the power would have to come from the Lord.

Ironically, the woman with all the offspring was the immature, selfish, and insensitive Peninnah. I feel sorry for her children. But Hannah, who would have made a tremendous mother, had no children. These two women illustrate that we cannot judge people by their outward circumstances. The work of God in a person's life goes much deeper than that.

The bitterness Hannah felt from Peninnah's mockery was an ongoing problem, not an isolated incident.

> And it happened year after year, as often as she went up to the house of the LORD, she would provoke her, so she wept and would not eat. Then Elkanah her husband said to her, "Hannah, why do you weep and why do you not eat and why is your heart sad? Am I not better to you than ten sons?" (1 Sam. 1:7, 8).

Elkanah was trying to make his wife look on the bright side. But he did more harm than good. He asked, "Why do you weep and why do you not eat and why is your heart sad?" Elkanah's threefold why shows that he did not understand his wife's problem. Instead of interrogating her, he should have wept with her. That would have shown compassion. But in essence he was telling Hannah to snap out of her depression, which is the best way to push a person deeper into the mire.

Hannah was the victim of three trials: She was unable to bear children; her husband had another wife (verse 6 calls her Hannah's rival) who rubbed salt into her emotional wound; and Hannah's husband did not understand her. These three trials produced three serious consequences: Hannah could not stop crying, she was unable to eat, and she was deeply depressed.

Maybe you know how that feels. Perhaps you've suffered these same symptoms. Many people in this predicament decide to take their own lives. Others retreat into an emotional shell. But Hannah was different. She allowed her trials to activate her prayer life. "And she, greatly distressed, prayed to the LORD and wept bitterly" (1 Sam. 1:10).

We've already seen the word *bitterly* in verse 6. And here it occurs again. Furthermore, the phrase *greatly distressed* in this verse means "bitter of soul" in Hebrew. Bitterness, then, had penetrated all the way down to Hannah's soul.

But she took it all to God in prayer, which reminds me of Joseph Scriven's hymn "What a Friend We Have in Jesus":

O what peace we often forfeit,
O what needless pain we bear,
All because we do not carry
Everything to God in prayer!

Hannah could have shouted back at Peninnah, lost her temper with her husband, and even resented God for closing her womb. But that would have made her trial go to waste. Instead, Hannah put her problem to good use. She allowed it to drive her to prayer. She was like Jesus in Gethsemane. Luke 22:44 tells us that while he was "in agony He was praying very fervently."

What is your trial? Are you letting it go to waste? Or are you using it as a point of leverage in your spiritual growth? Hannah took the right first step. But two more steps had to be taken to transform her bitterness into blessing.

Trust Accentuated Her Prayers

In Hannah's prayer the accent is on trusting God, not just for the birth of a son, but for his entire life.

> And she made a vow and said, "O LORD of hosts, if Thou wilt indeed look on the affliction of Thy maidservant and remember me, and not forget Thy maidservant, but wilt give Thy maidservant a son, then I will give him to the LORD all the days of his life, and a razor shall never come on his head" (1 Sam. 1:11).

At first glance Hannah's vow appears to be a deal she was striking up with God. "Lord, if you'll give me a son, I'll give him back to you!" God, of course, is not some celestial car salesman with whom we can bargain for blessings, and surely Hannah knew that. I don't think she was playing one-upmanship with the Lord.

She prayed for just one son, yet she was willing to surrender him to God. She only longed for the blessing so she might place it at the feet of her heavenly master. In this eleventh verse Hannah called herself the Lord's maidservant three times. Unlike Peninnah, she did not desire a son so she could mock other women who were sterile. Nor did she wish to throw a counter jab back at Peninnah and say, "She who laughs last, laughs best!" Her only motive was to yield her greatest treasure to God. And that proved her faith.

Now it came about, as she continued praying before the
LORD, that Eli was watching her mouth. As for Hannah,
she was speaking in her heart, only her lips were moving,
but her voice was not heard. So Eli thought she was drunk.
Then Eli said to her, "How long will you make yourself
drunk? Put away your wine from you" (1 Sam. 1:12–14).

Eli was guilty of the same mistake the crowds made
concerning the apostles when they were filled with the
Holy Spirit. The people accused them of being drunk
(Acts 2:13). And Ephesians 5:18 commands us, "Do not
get drunk with wine . . . but be filled with the Spirit."

Eli was the priest of God's people, yet when Hannah
was filled with the Spirit, he thought she was drunk. He
rebuked a godly woman when she was praying. How
insensitive! But our high priest, Jesus, never misunder-
stands us. He never discourages us in prayer or unfairly
rebukes us for it. Eli added to Hannah's burden, but Jesus
lifts ours.

Hannah was quick to explain to the mistaken priest:

"No, my lord, I am a woman oppressed in spirit; I have
drunk neither wine nor strong drink, but I have poured
out my soul before the LORD. Do not consider your maidservant as a worthless woman; for I have spoken until
now out of my great concern and provocation." Then Eli
answered and said, "Go in peace; and may the God of
Israel grant your petition that you have asked of Him."
And she said, "Let your maidservant find favor in your
sight." So the woman went her way and ate, and her face
was no longer sad (1 Sam. 1:15–18).

Here is another example of Hannah's trust in God. She
brought her burden to the Lord in prayer and left it there.
Eli did not give her absolute assurance of answered prayer.

He merely said, "May the God of Israel grant your petition that you have asked of Him." But that was all Hannah needed to hear. The brightness of joy burst out on her face, and the sadness disappeared. She was trusting in her generous God to give her the son for whom she had prayed.

A similar example occurred in the case of Monica, the mother of Augustine, back in the fourth century A.D. Before he was twenty, Augustine had a mistress who bore him an illegitimate son. He left his mother's home and moved in with this woman. Monica's heart broke. She was unconcerned about the result of this disgrace on her own reputation. All she cared about was her son's eternal welfare.

Augustine then joined a cult. As his contempt for his mother's Christian faith grew, so did Monica's prayers for her son. But for fourteen years Augustine continued to harden his heart. Finally Monica begged a minister to talk to her son and refute his errors. But the man of God replied that Augustine was unreachable. Monica refused to accept that. She then shed a flood of tears in front of him for her lost son.

Seeing that, the minister told Monica, "Go your way, and God bless you. For it is not possible that the son of these tears should perish."

Monica accepted those words as if they had been God's voice from heaven. She left encouraged and absolutely certain that Augustine would give his heart to Christ. And he did! More than that, he became perhaps the chief theologian between the apostle Paul of the first century and Martin Luther of the sixteenth. God honored Monica's faith.

Hannah's faith was also rewarded:

And Elkanah had relations with Hannah his wife, and the LORD remembered her. And it came about in due time, after Hannah had conceived, that she gave birth to a son; and she named him Samuel, saying, "Because I have asked him of the LORD" (1 Sam. 1:19, 20).

Some professing believers, if they had been Hannah, would have told the Lord, "Remember my prayer request for a son? Don't worry about that anymore. My infertility is finally over, and the problem has solved itself."

But Hannah was careful to give God the credit for answering her prayer. The name *Samuel* means "asked of God" or "heard by God." Every time she would call her boy by name, it would remind her that God had given him in answer to her prayer.

Eventually, Hannah fulfilled her vow.

Now when she had weaned him, she took him up with her . . . and brought him to the house of the LORD in Shiloh, although the child was young . . . and brought the boy to Eli. And she said, "Oh, my lord! As your soul lives, my lord, I am the woman who stood here beside you, praying to the LORD. For this boy I prayed, and the LORD has given me my petition which I asked of Him. So I have also dedicated him to the LORD; as long as he lives he is dedicated to the LORD." And he worshiped the LORD there (1 Sam. 1:24–28).

Try to comprehend how difficult this was for Hannah. Samuel was barely weaned, about three years old, and his mother would not be bringing him home. We know from 1 Samuel 2:12 that "the sons of Eli were worthless men; they did not know the LORD." They even committed open adultery (v. 22). And it was their father who would be raising Samuel. Hannah might have said, "Lord, when I made that vow to you, I didn't realize that Eli was such a poor father. Please understand that I can't leave Samuel with him. I must take my boy back home with me."

But she did not say that. She knew in her heart that she was giving Samuel to the Lord, not to Eli. God would watch over him in spite of Eli's reported negligence. That's faith. Hannah knew how to trust God.

Thanksgiving Accelerated Her Prayers

The second chapter of 1 Samuel opens with these words: "Then Hannah prayed and said . . . "(1 Sam. 2:1). What follows is a chorus of thanksgiving. In chapter 1 Hannah prayed without words (v. 13). But in chapter 2 she unleashed line after line of poetic praise in prayer.

She began by saying, "My heart exults in the LORD. . . . I rejoice in Thy salvation" (v. 1).

We would expect her to say, "My heart exults in Samuel, and I rejoice in being a mother." But instead, it was the Lord himself and his salvation that gladdened her heart. There was no trace of depression in Hannah's voice over giving Samuel to God. The Lord was truly her treasure.

She went on to tell him, "Indeed, there is no one besides Thee" (v. 2).

That's proof that Samuel had not become an idol to Hannah. Some parents place their children above Jesus in their affections. But Hannah had the Lord right where he belonged—in a class by himself. When God commanded Abraham to offer Isaac on the altar of sacrifice, he was testing the patriarch to see if his son was more important to him than his Lord. And like Hannah, Abraham passed his test with flying colors.

In verse 7 Hannah said, "The LORD makes poor and rich; He brings low, He also exalts."

Scripture is full of examples of people who were poor

and low, whom the Lord made spiritually rich and exalted.
Joseph, Moses, Mordecai, David, Daniel, Mary, and Jesus'
disciples illustrate this truth, as well as Hannah. Anyone
who is blessed has God to thank for it, and Hannah was
giving her thanks.

At the end of her prayer, Hannah said of the Lord, "He
will give strength to His king, and will exalt the horn of
His anointed" (1 Sam. 2:10).

Hannah spoke of the Lord's king. But this was about
fifty years before Israel's first king came to the throne. In
the next line she called this king the Lord's anointed. This
is the Hebrew word for "Messiah." It's the first mention of
the Messiah in the Bible. You and I know who he is. Talk
about accelerated prayer! In a state of prophecy, Hannah's
mind and heart advanced one thousand years into the
future, and she thanked God for Jesus Christ.

Personal Application

I see three main lessons we can gather from the prayer
life of Hannah. First, the purpose of prayer is to transform
us. Hannah's fervent request for a son did not convince an
unwilling God to open her womb. No doubt it was the
Lord's will all along to bring Samuel into this world.
What, then, did her prayer accomplish? It transformed
her heart. It was the spade that dug down to her bitterness, rooted it up, and planted joy in its place.

How much has prayer changed you? Has it increased
your trust in Christ? Has it inspired thanksgiving in your
heart? Has it set you free from bitterness? Has it quenched
your temper? If your praying has not changed you, it's not
a biblical prayer life you're practicing.

Next, Hannah teaches us that God honors prayer when
it seeks his glory above our personal interests. This woman

requested one son, that she might dedicate him to the Lord's service all his life. And God gave her Samuel. But later in the story we read that "the LORD visited Hannah; and she conceived and gave birth to three sons and two daughters" (1 Sam. 2:21). We expected the heavenly Father to turn her bitterness into blessing by letting her become the mother of Samuel. But he did so much more. He gave her five children in return for the one she gave him. And as if that weren't enough, he allowed her to utter a prophecy of the Messiah, Jesus Christ.

Do your prayers seem to bounce off the ceiling? Maybe James 4:3 expresses the reason: "You ask and do not receive, because you ask with wrong motives, so that you may spend it on your pleasures."

Finally, Hannah's prayer life reminds us that spiritual reproduction should be the heart's desire of every Christian. Perhaps like Hannah you are also sterile, but in a different sense. You have no spiritual children. You've never led anyone through the experience of new birth in Christ. Just as Peninnah mocked Hannah for her barrenness, so the world ridicules the church for believing in evangelism but not practicing it. God permits this ridicule because he wants us to grieve over our spiritual fruitlessness.

But sad to say, many Christians couldn't care less that they have failed to lead anyone through the spiritual birth canal of faith in Christ. Where is the anguish of Hannah? We should beg God to cure our infertility and make our churches maternity wards for the new birth. If Hannah's prayer life is any indication, and I think it is, God will delight to answer that prayer and do "exceeding abundantly beyond all that we ask or think" (Eph. 3:20).

When our failure in evangelism becomes a bitterness to us, God will turn it into the blessing of new life for many.

6

The Prayer Life of Samuel
Unceasing Fellowship with God

One of the shortest verses in the Bible tells us to "pray without ceasing" (1 Thess. 5:17). I think most Christians feel totally incapable of fulfilling that command. It sounds unreasonable, doesn't it? Not even monks living in a monastery can always be down on their knees with heads bowed and eyes closed. We know from the Book of Acts that Paul himself, who penned these words, was not always uttering prayers.

So what does this verse mean? It speaks of living in a constant attitude of prayer. Suppose a young woman goes to bed early. Later that night her husband enters the bedroom and asks her a question. But she's sound asleep and doesn't hear him. The husband then turns the radio on, and his wife still doesn't stir. But at two o'clock in the morning, the baby lets out a tiny whimper. Instantly the young mother is awake. All night long she had been listening carefully for her child, even though her mind was dead to the rest of the world.

To pray without ceasing is to be listening for God and communicating with him, even when you are involved in other matters. An outstanding example of someone who prayed without ceasing is Samuel, the last and greatest of Israel's judges. On one occasion his people pled with him, "Do not cease to cry to the LORD our God for us" (1 Sam. 7:8). And in his retirement speech later in life he told them, "Far be it from me that I should sin against the LORD by ceasing to pray for you" (1 Sam. 12:23). Samuel enjoyed unceasing fellowship with God.

He Was Nurtured in Prayer

As the First Book of Samuel opens, we meet a woman named Hannah. She was brokenhearted over being child-less. So she poured out her soul to God, wept bitterly, and prayed for a son. The Lord granted her request, and she named her boy Samuel, which means "asked of God." Every time he introduced himself to others by name later in life, he would be reminded that he was born in answer to prayer. Often when I meet someone named Samuel, I wonder if he, too, came into this world in answer to his parents' prayers.

First Samuel 1:24 says Hannah "brought him to the house of the LORD in Shiloh, although the child was young." And as an act of dedication to God, she left him there with Eli the priest. A woman of prayer placed her son in a house of prayer, and he became a man of prayer.

I believe the church is a seedbed for spiritual life. If you want to grow a beautiful flower, you plant it in a properly prepared piece of ground, where it will be watered and nurtured. A flower might also grow in a dry weed patch, but its chance of survival is much greater in a seedbed. Do you want your children to know, love, and serve Christ? Then put them under spiritual influences, one of which is the church. Young people who are nurtured in a house of prayer are the most likely to become men and women of prayer. Of course the home should also be a spiritual training ground. But in the church children will see people of all ages and walks of life who love Christ and are serving him. Samuels are usually trained—though not always—from birth.

In the third chapter of 1 Samuel, God spoke to the boy. Three times he called Samuel by name. But the child had never heard the Lord's voice, so he thought Eli was calling him. After the third time, Eli realized it was God addressing Samuel. So he told his young apprentice to reply:

> "Speak, LORD, for Thy servant is listening." So Samuel went and lay down in his place. Then the LORD came and stood and called as at other times, "Samuel! Samuel!" And Samuel said, "Speak, for Thy servant is listening" (1 Sam. 3:9, 10).

The boy answered exactly as Eli had instructed him, except he left out the word LORD. Some think this was because he wasn't sure who was speaking to him. But there is a better explanation. In Hebrew "LORD" is the personal name for God, *Yahweh,* sometimes pronounced "Jehovah." Out of reverence for God, the Jews would not dare utter this name. So we see that even in his boyhood, Samuel was reverent in prayer.

All four times God spoke to him during that night, Samuel was lying on his bed. Like that young mother who was listening for the cries of her baby even in her sleep, Samuel had ears for the Lord. Many of us sleep through

our prayers and sleep instead of pray. But Samuel jumped
out of his bed when it was time to talk to God. The training and example of his mother and Eli the priest nurtured
him in prayer.

He Was Victorious in Prayer

The next time we find Samuel in prayer, he was calling
the nation of Israel to repentance. He told them to put
away their idols and serve the Lord alone. The people
agreed to do that, so the man of God called for a national
day of prayer: "Then Samuel said, 'Gather all Israel to
Mizpah, and I will pray to the LORD for you'" (1 Sam. 7:5).

The child of prayer had become a man of prayer. He was
the leader of a tremendous revival in Israel. On this day of
prayer God's people fasted and confessed their sins. The
Philistines, however, heard about this gathering and as-
sumed it was for the purpose of making war against them.
They did not understand prayer meetings, so they attacked
the Israelites.

The lesson here is that whenever we recommit ourselves
to Christ, our enemy Satan will launch an assault against
us. He always wages war against revival in our lives.

When the people of Israel saw the Philistines coming,
they said to Samuel:

> "Do not cease to cry to the LORD our God for us, that He
> may save us from the hand of the Philistines." And Samuel
> took a suckling lamb and offered it for a whole burnt offer-
> ing to the LORD; and Samuel cried to the LORD for Israel
> and the LORD answered him (1 Sam. 7:8, 9).

While Samuel was praying, he offered a sacrifice to the
Lord. For us that means we must present our prayers in the
name of Christ, who was sacrificed for our sins on the cross.

A well-meaning Christian once remarked to Donald Barnhouse, "I believe in prayer." Barnhouse was quick to reply, "I don't. I believe in God, who answers prayer." He then used the analogy of a person who believes in writing checks. What if he has no account in the bank? He can take his check up to the teller, write it out to cash, sign it, and hand it in. But he's not going to get any money.

In the same way, prayer is valuable only if we offer it in Jesus' name. He's the one who has an account of righteousness in heaven's bank. Jews, Muslims, Buddhists, and others pray to God, but not through Christ. If prayer had its own intrinsic power, it would make no difference whether we approached God through Jesus, some other mediator, or in our own name. Even Samuel in the Old Testament teaches us that the heavenly Father can only be appealed to on the basis of sacrifice. And Scripture is clear that the sacrifice that pleases him is the shed blood of Jesus on the cross.

See what God did in response to Samuel's prayer and sacrifice: "The LORD thundered with a great thunder on that day against the Philistines and confused them, so that they were routed before Israel" (1 Sam. 7:10).

This was a supernatural victory. There were no swords, spears, bows, or arrows involved. Still today the only weapon that brings victory in our spiritual warfare against Satan is the miraculous power of God. And that is unleashed through prayer in Christ's name.

He Was Encouraged in Prayer

A bit later on the people of Israel told Samuel they wanted to have a king to rule over them, just as did the other nations. "But the thing was displeasing in the sight of Samuel when they said, 'Give us a king to judge us'" (1 Sam. 8:6).

Few things hurt more than being rejected by someone you love. For many years Samuel had served Israel faithfully and interceded with God for them. And now they were telling him, "We want a king to take your place."

If I had been Samuel, I probably would have reminded these people of all I had done for them. I would have demanded to know why they were calling for my resignation. I might have even defied their request and required them to fire me. But Samuel didn't argue, complain, cry, challenge, or rebuke his people. Instead, "Samuel prayed to the LORD" (1 Sam. 8:6).

Are you being rejected by someone you love? Instead of feeling depressed and sorry for yourself, pray about it. The Lord has some lesson for you to learn in this experience. And he also wants to be your comforter. Joseph Scriven put it this way in his hymn, "What a Friend We Have in Jesus":

> Do thy friends despise, forsake thee?
> Take it to the Lord in prayer!
> In His arms He'll take and shield thee;
> Thou wilt find a solace there.

After Samuel prayed, God told him to give the people what they wanted, then encouraged him with these words: "They have not rejected you, but they have rejected Me from being king over them" (1 Sam. 8:7). Hearing that, Samuel was able to put away personal bitterness. Prayer had helped him see his personal crisis from God's point of view.

The Lord also instructed Samuel to warn the people that a king would take their sons for war, their lands for his own use, their servants for his work, and themselves as his slaves. This warning was intended to change the minds of the Israelites. But they replied, "No, but there shall be a king over us" (1 Sam. 8:19).

And this is how Samuel handled his frustration: "Now after Samuel had heard all the words of the people, he repeated them in the LORD's hearing" (1 Sam. 8:21).

Of course God already knew what Israel had said. Samuel's prayer, therefore, was for his own benefit rather than the Lord's. It served as an outlet for unloading his sorrows. It relieved him of bitterness. And it gave him a fresh outlook on his problem, one from which he could see God's viewpoint. That's how prayer can encourage us today.

He Was Persuasive in Prayer

Later, during wheat harvest, Samuel was standing before his people. It was the middle of the summer when rain was rare, and there were no threatening clouds in the sky that day. Samuel spoke up and said:

> "Is it not the wheat harvest today? I will call to the LORD, that He may send thunder and rain. Then you will know and see that your wickedness is great which you have done in the sight of the LORD by asking for yourselves a king." So Samuel called to the LORD, and the LORD sent thunder and rain that day; and all the people greatly feared the LORD and Samuel (1 Sam. 12:17, 18).

The thunder and rain were striking visual aids that illustrated the sin of Israel. They felt secure with their new king, Saul. But Samuel was showing them that their condition could change as quickly as the weather during wheat harvest. No one expected the wheat harvest to be ruined by rain on a beautiful summer afternoon. Nor did they expect to see their nation defeated, now that they had a king. But the harvest was damaged, and Israel would also be overrun by the Philistines.

Samuel's prayer brought results. The thunder roared, the

rain flooded the ground, and the people confessed their guilt before God.

There is a name for what the people experienced: conviction. Today it occurs when people sense their guilt before a holy God, confess their sins, and trust Jesus Christ to make them new. Many people you and I know need to be under conviction and aren't. We can witness to them and even preach to them. But apart from prayer, neither of those things will pierce their hearts. Sometimes we resort to even less spiritual methods of convicting people, like arguing and nagging. Unlike Samuel, we cannot call down thunder and rain from the sky. But like him, our prayers can be a tool God uses for persuading people of their need for Christ.

Many a wife has been limited to prayer for a husband who refused to let her talk about faith in Jesus. The same is true of children whose parents are hardened toward the gospel. Every line of communication regarding spiritual truth has been severed—except the prayer line, which is the most effective line of all. God is able to change the hearts of people who have no intention of changing. The job of persuasion can be performed only by him. And he persuades in response to the prayers of his children.

He Was Loving in Prayer

The beginning of King Saul's reign is recorded in 1 Samuel 13. Immediately before that Samuel gave his retirement speech. He was about to step down from his office as judge of Israel. Although the people had sinned in asking for a king, Samuel refused to carry a grudge against them. Instead, he said, "Moreover, as for me, far be it from me that I should sin against the LORD by ceasing to pray for you" (1 Sam. 12:23).

Samuel loved his nation too much to cease praying for

it. He couldn't help himself. For him it would have been a sin to quit interceding for others.

And the same is true for us. We often think of sin as some bad thing we do. But James 4:17 makes it clear that sin is also a good thing we leave undone. First Timothy 2:1, 3, 4 says: "First of all, then, I urge that entreaties and prayers, petitions and thanksgivings, be made on behalf of all men. . . . This is good and acceptable in the sight of God our Savior, who desires all men to be saved and to come to the knowledge of the truth."

Put simply, the Word of God commands us to pray for others, that they might find salvation in Christ. Are you doing that? If not, or if you have ceased in that activity, you are sinning against God. Intercessory prayer is the most loving act we can do for other people.

First Samuel 15:10, 11 gives us another example of Samuel's love in prayer:

> Then the word of the LORD came to Samuel, saying, "I regret that I have made Saul king, for he has turned back from following Me, and has not carried out My commands." And Samuel was distressed and cried out to the LORD all night.

If Samuel had been selfish, he might have said, "Hallelujah! Now that Saul is being rejected, I'm going to get my old job back. That ought to show those people for demanding a king!"

But instead of that, Samuel was distressed and cried out to the Lord all night. I wonder what he said to God in prayer. Maybe it was something like this: "O Lord, I can't stand to see Saul cut off from you. Have mercy on him. Please, please, don't let this happen. Discipline Saul if you must, but don't reject him. O Lord, no!"

That's how we should pray when we think of people getting rejected on the judgment day. Does the thought of your worst enemy going to hell cheer you, or does it break your heart? Are you concerned for the lost, or have you lost your concern?

The apostle Paul was persecuted by the first-century Jews. They made false accusations against him, called for his execution, and even had him stoned. Yet he could say of them, "I have great sorrow and unceasing grief in my heart. For I could wish that I myself were accursed, separated from Christ for the sake of my brethren, my kinsmen according to the flesh" (Rom. 9:2, 3). Paul was willing to forfeit his salvation and go to hell if only the Jews would trust and love Christ.

God takes no delight in the condemnation of people, nor should we. If Christ could shed his blood on Calvary's cross to save people, we can intercede for them. Jesus prayed that the heavenly Father would forgive His murderers (Luke 23:34). So there is no excuse for our failing to pray for our worst enemies. It's the most loving thing we can do, and love is the foremost commandment in the Bible (Mark 12:30, 31).

He Was Famous in Prayer

There are two passages outside the book of First Samuel in which further attention is called to this man's prayer life. One is Psalm 99:6:

> Moses and Aaron were among His priests,
> And Samuel was among those who called on His name;
> They called upon the LORD, and He answered them.

Samuel is in good company along with Moses, the most famous Old Testament character, and Aaron, the first high priest. But don't overlook that word *among*. The psalmist is not putting these men in a class by themselves. They were "among those who called on His name." So there is a place for other prayer warriors. I can name many today, and you could be one of them.

The prophet Jeremiah, also, calls attention to Samuel's outstanding prayer life: "Then the LORD said to me, 'Even though Moses and Samuel were to stand before Me, My heart would not be with this people; send them away from My presence and let them go!'" (Jer. 15:1).

By this time Israel had become so ripe for judgment that not even the intercessory prayers of Moses and Samuel would prevail for it. But what I want you to see here is that when God mentioned two great men of prayer to Jeremiah, Samuel was one of them.

Do you have a reputation for prayer? I think the best way to judge that is to recall how many times others have asked you to intercede with God for them. Do you receive regular phone calls and other requests asking for prayer? If so, that's a good sign that your prayer life has touched other people. God is using you.

Personal Application

Samuel shows us what it means to live in an attitude of prayer. He was nurtured in prayer, victorious in prayer, encouraged in prayer, persuasive in prayer, loving in prayer, and famous in prayer. To pray without ceasing, therefore, is to saturate every area of life with appeals to God, to consider him in every decision, and to live in his presence.

Perhaps that would require a total change in your life. But that only means you need to change. God is willing to help you change. Are you willing? No lifestyle is more satisfying than that of enjoying unceasing fellowship with God.

7

The Prayer Life of Elijah
Expecting Results from the Lord

In the past three months you've probably voiced more prayer requests than you can count. Wonderful! But perhaps you can't add up your answers to prayer, either, not because there are too many, but because you can't pinpoint any.

I struggle with this, too. Sometimes the reason is that we make a vague request. If God did send us an answer, we wouldn't know it because the petition was not specific enough in the first place.

More often, we receive no results from our prayers because we don't expect them. Sometimes we humbly kneel before God, remind him of a promise he made in Scripture, ask him to fulfill it, and thank him in advance for the sure answer. Then we rise to our feet and say in our hearts, "It will never be mine." James 1:8 calls the person who does this "a double-minded man, unstable in all his ways."

When the prophet Elijah voiced requests to the Lord, he expected results and received them. His prayer life illustrates four specific results we can anticipate from God in our prayer lives.

Expect the Lord to Resurrect the Dead

Early in Elijah's ministry God led him to Zarephath, where the prophet performed a miracle that kept a widow and her son from starving to death. But later the boy fell sick and died. The grief-stricken mother informed Elijah.

> He said to her, "Give me your son." Then he took him from her bosom and carried him up to the upper room where he was living, and laid him on his own bed. And he called to the LORD and said, "O LORD my God, hast Thou also brought calamity to the widow with whom I am staying, by causing her son to die?" Then he stretched himself upon the child three times, and called to the LORD, and said, "O LORD my God, I pray Thee, let this child's life return to him" (1 Kings 17:19–21).

If I had been Elijah, I think I would have prayed like this: "Lord, please comfort this dear woman's heart in her time of loss. Minister to her through your Spirit." But the prophet's plea was bold: "Let this child's life return to him." Under any circumstances, that would be a daring request. But it was doubly so, because at this point in history no one had ever returned from the dead.

When we read this story with New Testament understanding, we see that the child who died represents people who have not trusted Christ as their personal Savior. They are spiritually dead. Ephesians 2:1, 5 is clear: "And you were dead in your trespasses and sins. . . . We were dead in our transgressions."

Do you believe that people who don't know Jesus are dead? Does the thought of them spending eternity in hell cause the hair on your neck to stand on end? What if Elijah had told the grieving widow, "Your son isn't dead; he's just sleeping"? The boy would never have enjoyed life again. And if you and I take lightly the horror of spiritual death, many people we know and love will perish in hell forever.

What, then, should we do? Elijah's example offers us three clues. First, he placed the corpse on his own bed. When guests visit your home, you invite them to sit on a couch or chair in the living room, not on your bed in the bedroom. A bed is too personal for that. Yet Elijah laid a corpse, of all things, on his bed.

I believe God is telling us he wants unconverted people to lie on the bed of our hearts. Our tendency is to reserve that spot for our plans, our desires, and our cherished dreams. The disturbing thought of a lost soul is not likely to make it past the heavily guarded gate of our hearts. But is that right? Dare we be comfortable when others are perishing? The prominent reason we don't win unbelievers to Christ is that they are not lying on the beds of our hearts.

After Elijah placed the corpse on his bed, he "stretched" himself on it three times. As an adult, Elijah was taller than the child. We would expect that when he placed his body on the boy's, he would have contracted himself. Instead, he stretched while he prayed.

We need to stretch ourselves in prayer for the lost. We've failed to pray with passion. We've shed no tears. Our hearts have not broken. Elijah placed his body on top of the boy's. But we have not identified ourselves with people who are dead in sin. Our hearts have not touched their hearts. Their predicament hasn't become ours. Instead, we've been distant. This is why God has been unable to use us to resurrect spiritually dead people to newness of life in Christ. When we should be stretching, we are slackening.

Once we've placed nonbelievers on the beds of our hearts and have stretched ourselves in prayer for them, we must then expect our Lord to give them life. Elijah had perfect confidence that God would put breath into this child's body. And sure enough, "the LORD heard the voice of Elijah, and the life of the child returned to him and he revived" (1 Kings 17:22).

If Elijah could trust God for a physical resurrection, can't we trust him to bring about a spiritual resurrection for people who are dead in their sins? I think that faith in the latter is easier, don't you?

But right there we show our weakness. When someone does give his or her heart to Christ, we are surprised. We read in Scripture that God "desires all men to be saved and to come to the knowledge of the truth" (1 Tim. 2:4) and that he is "not wishing for any to perish but for all to come to repentance" (2 Peter 3:9). But still we do not expect to see people converted. And that's why they are not. As Jesus said, "Be it done to you according to your faith" (Matt. 9:29).

Occasionally the heavenly Father will encourage our weak faith. Not long ago a stranger came to my office to ask a personal favor of me. Introducing himself, he told me about his church background. I replied, "Does that mean you've invited Jesus Christ into your heart as your personal Savior?" Quickly he answered, "No, sir."

I was surprised and pursued his reasons why. After I cleared up his misconceptions about the new birth, I asked him if he would like to receive Christ. When he said yes, I could hardly believe it! I had just met the man fifteen minutes earlier. As I look back on that, I think God was teaching my skeptical heart to expect lost people to say yes to the gospel. After all, it *is* good news.

Expect the Lord to Revive the Church

Elijah's next recorded prayer took place during his celebrated contest with the prophets of Baal on Mount Carmel. He had proposed that two altars be set up. First his adversaries would pray for Baal to send fire from heaven on their altar. Then he would make the same request of the Lord. And the god who answered by fire would be the true God. The false prophets agreed, but saw no response to their all-day ranting and raving.

Then Elijah set up his altar, drenched it with water, and offered this simple prayer:

> "O LORD, the God of Abraham, Isaac and Israel, today let it be known that Thou art God in Israel, and that I am Thy servant, and that I have done all these things at Thy word. Answer me, O LORD, answer me, that this people may know that Thou, O LORD, art God, and that Thou hast turned their heart back again" (1 Kings 18:36, 37).

The nation of Israel was God's chosen people. But in Elijah's day they had grown indifferent. They had lost their love for the Lord. They were worshiping Baal. They desperately needed revival.

And that's precisely what Elijah prayed for. He asked that the fire would fall "so these people will know that You are God and You have brought them back to Yourself" (v. 37 LB).

The word *revival* is made up of two Latin roots: *re* meaning "again," and *vivere* meaning "to be alive." Revival applies to the revitalizing of something that used to be alive but is now decaying. Someone has defined it as "the inrush of the Holy Spirit into the body that threatens to become a corpse." That is the great need of the body of Christ, the church. How many times have you heard of a dead church? Too many local congregations, as well as the members who make them up, show no signs of life.

In his book *Revivals of Religion* Charles Finney offers these seven signs of a church that is in need of revival: First is a lack of brotherly love among believers. Second, division, jealousy, and gossip are prominent. Third, a worldly spirit enters the church. Fourth, some of its members fall into gross and scandalous sins. Fifth, arguments break out between the members. Sixth, nonbelievers justly criticize the church. And seventh, the damnation of the lost fails to stir believers to action.

Does that describe our spiritual condition? I think it fits many churches today. As a result, we should be praying for revival.

Many of us are pleading with God for revival, yet revival hasn't come. Why? I believe it is because we desire revival for the glory it will bring to us or our congregations. We want people to say, "Have you heard about the outpouring of the Holy Spirit in their church?" That sounds impressive. It makes us look like we have a corner on God. But the Lord cannot trust proud people with a revival. Before God opens the floodgates of heaven, we must be willing for the showers of blessing to fall someplace other than where we are. We must be eager for God to bless anyone, any place, any church—including those with whom we disagree doctrinally and with whom we compete.

If Elijah had been a slave to his human nature, he would

have asked God to send fire from heaven "so these people will know that I am one powerful prophet." Instead, he prayed, "Answer me, O LORD, answer me, that this people may know that Thou, O LORD, art God, and that Thou hast turned their heart back again." Those words prove that Elijah had overcome the fierce enemy of selfishness. This was the result:

> The fire of the LORD fell, and consumed the burnt offering and the wood and the stones and the dust, and licked up the water that was in the trench. And when all the people saw it, they fell on their faces; and they said, "The LORD, He is God; the LORD, He is God" (1 Kings 18:38, 39).

God gave Israel the revival Elijah prayed for and expected. We, also, can pray expectantly, but only when personal pride has been crucified and all our yearning is for the glory of our Lord Jesus.

Expect the Lord to Require Perseverance

Shortly after the contest on Mount Carmel, Elijah told this to Israel's King Ahab:

> "Go up, eat and drink; for there is the sound of the roar of a heavy shower." So Ahab went up to eat and drink. But Elijah went up to the top of Carmel; and he crouched down on the earth, and put his face between his knees. And he said to his servant, "Go up now, look toward the sea." So he went up and looked and said, "There is nothing." And he said, "Go back" seven times. And it came about at the seventh time, that he said, "Behold, a cloud as small as a man's hand is coming up from the sea." And he said, "Go up, say to Ahab, 'Prepare your chariot and go down, so that the heavy shower does not stop you.'" So it

came about in a little while, that the sky grew black with
clouds and wind, and there was a heavy shower (1 Kings
18:41–45).

Commenting on this event, the New Testament tells us
that Elijah "prayed . . . and the sky poured rain" (James
5:18). For three and a half years the clouds had not yielded
a drop. Famine had swept over the land of Israel because
of the people's apostasy. But they had just confessed with
their mouths that "the LORD, He is God" (1 Kings 18:39).
So now the blessing could flow.

Earlier in the Book of First Kings, Solomon anticipated
this circumstance. He prayed: "When the heavens are shut
up and there is no rain, because they have sinned against
Thee, and they pray toward this place and confess Thy
name and turn from their sin . . . then hear in heaven and
forgive the sin of . . . Israel. . . . And send rain on Thy
land" (1 Kings 8:35, 36). That prayer gave Elijah the right
to ask for rain, because Israel had fulfilled the conditions.

But even then the Lord did not answer immediately, and
Elijah had to persevere. While crouched in prayer, the
prophet was positive dark clouds would be forming. So he
sent his servant to look for them. But the report came
back, "I don't see a thing." Six times Elijah said, "Look out
over the sea," and six times his servant replied, "There isn't
a cloud in the sky." We don't know how long Elijah cried
out to God each time before he sent his servant back to
look again. The entire process might have taken hours. But
he persevered.

Genuine faith can wait for God. Jacob did not receive
his blessing until he had wrestled all night with the Lord
(Gen. 32:24–26). George Müller endured in prayer for
sixty–three years for a friend's conversion. That friend
finally gave his heart to Christ at Müller's funeral.

If you cannot think of a prayer request that God has delayed answering, then you simply are not praying. It may be the salvation of a family member, freedom from an alcohol or drug addiction for yourself or someone you know, the healing of a broken marriage, or reconciliation between two feuding Christians. You've begged God to step in and act in these or similar situations, but so far he has been silent.

Charles Spurgeon has an encouraging comment here:

> If you are sure it is a right thing for which you are asking, plead now, plead at noon, plead at night, plead on. With cries and tears spread out your case. Order your arguments. Back up your pleas with reasons. Urge the precious blood of Jesus. Set the wounds of Christ before the Father's eyes. Bring out the atoning sacrifice. Point to Calvary. Enlist the crowned Prince, the Priest who stands at the right hand of God. And resolve in your very soul that if souls be not saved, if your family be not blessed, if your own zeal be not revived, yet you will die with the plea on your lips, and with the importunate wish on your spirits (*Spurgeon At His Best*, [Baker, 1988] pp. 151, 152).

If even the mighty prayer warrior Elijah had to persevere in prayer, can we expect to snap our fingers and have the Lord at our beck and call? Certainly not. What we can expect is that the heavenly Father will require steadfast endurance as we appeal to Him. We must learn not only to wait *on* God, but to wait *for* Him.

Expect the Lord to Refuse Some of Your Requests

Elijah's final prayer recorded in Scripture is a pitiful one. The wicked Queen Jezebel wanted him dead, not alive, so she placed a bounty on his head. You would not think that would faze a man who had just called down fire from heaven. We might rather expect Elijah to have marched into Jezebel's palace and said with a wide grin, "Now let's see who can kill whom!" Instead, he ran in fear for his life—into the wilderness. "He requested for himself that he might die, and said, 'It is enough; now, O LORD, take my life'" (1 Kings 19:4).

Elijah had just fled from Jezebel because he did not want to die, and then he begged God to let him die! Obviously his depression affected his ability to reason. And in love the Lord denied his request.

Little did the prophet realize that God would someday send a chariot of fire to escort him straight from earth into heaven without his dying. If Elijah's last prayer request had been granted, he would have deprived himself of an experience that is unparalleled in Scripture. This was surely one petition he later thanked God for refusing.

Never was I more frightened of a teacher than of the one who kept me after school for long periods of time every day because I was not finishing my math assignments. My problem was that I didn't understand them. But the stern teacher accepted no excuses. In my childhood faith I begged God and my parents to transfer me into the other classroom of my grade. My parents saw the stress I was under, so they made the request for me to the principal.

Rather than grant it, the principal informed my teacher of my anxiety and fear. From then on she went out of her way to help me personally in class. Soon I was learning again, and that year I grew to love my teacher. The Lord answered my prayer the tough way—not by giving me an escape from my problem, but by transforming my problem into a dear friend. By the end of the year I was overflowing with thanks for God's refusal of my prayer request. And many times since then he has taught me that same lesson.

In our prayer lives we are like children learning to fill in a coloring book. They have two basic problems. First, they cannot keep within the boundary lines; second, they often choose the wrong colors. They may give a woman green hair or make a cow yellow. In our spiritual immaturity, we ask God for things that either transgress the guidelines of his will or are improper. This is why the Bible says, "We do not know how to pray as we should" (Rom. 8:26). Therefore, we must expect the Lord to refuse some of our requests. Even Elijah didn't get everything he prayed for—and all because God was loving.

Personal Application

In the New Testament we read that "the effective prayer of a righteous man can accomplish much" (James 5:16). The verse that follows cites Elijah as a case in point. We tend to think of him as a superman with a nature unlike ours. But no, "Elijah was a man with a nature like ours" (James 5:17). He was one of us, just an ordinary man. But when he prayed, extraordinary things happened.

James says the secret to Elijah's effective prayer life was that he was "righteous." And so are you, if you are trusting in Jesus as your personal Savior.

What, then, hinders you from receiving specific answers to your prayers? What particular thing does God want you to expect from him? For what is he asking you to believe him? The conversion of someone to whom you're witnessing? A love that is desperately needed in your family life? The blessing of the Holy Spirit that is missing in your church? Perhaps it's the ability to forgive someone who can never make amends for the hurt he or she has caused you.

Or possibly God wants you to trust his wisdom when he refuses your specific request.

If Elijah's prayer life teaches us anything, it's that we can expect to see these kinds of results from a living, loving, and almighty Lord.

8

The Prayer Life of Jehoshaphat

Looking to the Lord When You Don't Know What to Do

Often when people seek my counsel regarding personal problems, I have no concrete answers for them. What do you tell a mother whose heart is breaking because her teenage son doesn't love Christ, has no interest in spiritual things, and refuses to go with her to church? I suggested that she insist he at least attend church with her. But she replied, "What am I supposed to do—wrestle him out the door? He's bigger than I am. And if I tell him he must come to church or move out of my house, he'll move in with his girlfriend." I finally agreed that other than look to God in prayer for her son, there was nothing she could do.

What do you tell a husband whose wife says she no longer loves him and refuses to go to counseling? I gave him all the standard answers: love her unconditionally, be patient, and do not retaliate against her. But unless the Lord changes the heart of that wife, there really is nothing more the husband can do. His only real option is to look to the Lord and wait on him.

There are many times in our lives when we simply do not know what to do. I don't think we should be ashamed of that. Instead, we should take it as a reminder that in every situation we are at the mercy of God.

In the twentieth chapter of Second Chronicles we read of a man who had no idea what he could do or should do in his hour of crisis. He was Jehoshaphat, the fourth king of Judah, who reigned in the ninth century B.C. This narrative presents us with instructive lessons from his prayer life.

He Showed Intensity in Prayer

The opening of 2 Chronicles 20 sets the stage:

> Now it came about after this that the sons of Moab and the sons of Ammon, together with some of the Meunites, came to make war against Jehoshaphat. Then some came and reported to Jehoshaphat, saying, "A great multitude is coming against you from beyond the sea, out of Aram and behold, they are in Hazazon-tamar (that is Engedi)." And Jehoshaphat was afraid (vv. 1–3).

We have no clue as to why these other nations decided to attack Jehoshaphat. All the text says is that the odds were three against one—three nations, that is, against one man. They formed "a great multitude." That phrase occurs three times in this chapter. And it left the king shivering in fear for his life.

So what did he do? He "turned his attention to seek the LORD; and proclaimed a fast throughout all Judah"(v. 3).

Other kings would have said, "This is a time to fight, not pray. I need to seek a solution, not seek the Lord." But Jehoshaphat was true to his faith, even in an emergency. And he didn't merely tip his hat to God by mouthing a surface prayer. He *sought* the Lord. That word speaks of intensity in prayer. The biblical writer later summarizes Jehoshaphat's life by saying he "sought the LORD with all his heart" (2 Chron. 22:9).

Seeking implies exploration, and that's not easy. I'm the type of person who has everything organized, and if I misplace something and have to seek it, I easily become impatient. We live in the age of fast food, drive-through banking, and telecommunications, all of which make us hunger for instant gratification, even in our prayer lives. But Jesus told us not only to ask in prayer, but also to seek and knock (Matt. 7:7).

When the people of Judah saw Jehoshaphat's example, they "gathered together to seek help from the LORD; they even came from all the cities of Judah to seek the LORD" (2 Chron. 20:4).

Underscore the word *seek*, found twice in that verse. God was honoring the king's intensity in prayer by letting his seeking attitude rub off on his people.

He Used Logical Arguments in Prayer

From verses five through twelve Jehoshaphat stood before the men, women, and children of Judah and led them in prayer. In it he employed four logical arguments to enlist God's help. He was appealing to Jehovah on the basis of the following reasons:

The Rule of God

Jehoshaphat began his prayer with these words: "O
LORD, the God of our fathers, art Thou not God in the
heavens? And art Thou not ruler over all the kingdoms of
the nations?" (v. 6).

The king reminded the Lord that he was not merely a
faraway God in heaven but also the ruler of nations here
on earth. Jehoshaphat was saying, "You, Lord, are the
only one who is able to do something about the danger
we are in."

The Irresistible Power of God

At the end of verse 6 this man of prayer told the Lord,
"Power and might are in Thy hand so that no one can
stand against Thee."

Jehoshaphat believed that his enemies were no match
for the Lord. He knew that God could turn them into
friends, or he could bring them down in defeat in the time
of battle. Either way, they could not stand against his Lord.

Do you believe God is able to change people who don't
want to be changed? I do. He has his ways of changing the
minds, beliefs, and lives of even the most hardened athe-
ists. I'm not saying that God saves people against their
wills. I'm saying that he has his ways of making us willing.
He knows how to change our minds.

The apostle Paul is a case in point. On the day of his
conversion he had no intention of submitting to Christ. He
was breathing threats of murder against the Christians. But
in one moment Jesus turned Paul around, and from then
on his heart belonged to the Lord.

You may be married to an unbeliever. You've tried to
share your faith with him or her, but it has placed a strain

on your relationship. You've learned that there is nothing you can do. In times like that, don't forget what Jehoshaphat said: "No one can stand against Thee." If the Lord should only give the order, that unbelieving husband of yours would bow his head and pray, "God be merciful to me, the sinner."

One evening years ago I visited a man named Roy whose wife attended our church. I shared Christ with him but found him to be a proud unbeliever. He told me that Christianity was only for women, children, and weaklings. As I drove away from his house that night, I looked up and said, "Heavenly Father, I couldn't get to first base with Roy. But I'm not giving up on him. I know you can change his heart from the inside out."

Two or three days later Roy called me on the phone. His voice was full of joy as he told me he had trusted Jesus Christ as his personal Savior. Soon after that he was baptized, and he became a responsible member of our church. Not even he in all his stubborn pride could stand against God.

The Promises of God

Jehoshaphat went on to remind the Lord of two promises he had made, both of which were being threatened by the invasion of the three enemies. First, the king asked, "Didst Thou not, O our God, drive out the inhabitants of this land before Thy people Israel, and give it to the descendants of Abraham Thy friend forever?" (v. 7).

Yes, God had done exactly that. But if the three nations that were coming up against Jehoshaphat should conquer him and his people, the ownership of the land would change hands. And that would annul the divine promise.

Jehoshaphat reminded the Lord of a second promise:

"And they lived in it, and have built Thee a sanctuary there
for Thy name, saying, 'Should evil come upon us, the
sword, or judgment, or pestilence, or famine, we will stand
before this house and before Thee (for Thy name is in this
house) and cry to Thee in our distress, and Thou wilt hear
and deliver us'" (vv. 8, 9).

The king was quoting from Solomon's dedication prayer
after the temple had been built. In it a promise had been
given of protection from the same kind of danger Jehoshaphat and his people were in. By reminding the Lord of
his promise, the king was confident of securing the help he
needed.

Every so often my children will remind me of a promise
I've made earlier—maybe to take them for a walk or out to
eat or to play with them in the backyard. I confess that I'm
not always thrilled when they refresh my memory on
these things, but it is an effective way for a child to corner
a parent.

God, however, loves to be cornered. We honor him by
taking his promises seriously and expecting him to fulfill
them.

Do you require wisdom for an important decision that
lies ahead? Then claim the promise of James 1:5: "But if any
of you lacks wisdom, let him ask of God, who gives to all
men generously and without reproach, and it will be given
to him."

Maybe you have doubts that you truly belong to Christ.
Then read 1 John 5:11–13. It says that people who believe
in Christ may know they possess eternal life. Doubt of
God's promise is the only thing that keeps you from having
the assurance of your salvation. Why not take the Lord at
his Word? King Jehoshaphat was able to stand on the
promises when his life was on the line.

The Powerlessness of Man

In 2 Chronicles 20:12 we find the heart of the king's prayer. First, he admitted, "we are powerless before this great multitude."

The trouble with us is that we don't see ourselves as powerless against our enemy. We think we can fight temptation, sin, and the devil in our own strength. And that's a fatal deception. Often I hear Christians lament, "I wish I were stronger, so I could be more victorious over sin." What they really need, however, is to become not stronger but weaker. As long as we think we have one ounce of strength, we will try to use it. We will march into spiritual warfare dressed in nothing more than the nakedness of human will power. But every time we do that, we take a beating. Only when we acknowledge our total weakness will we rely completely on the power of the indwelling Christ. And only that will bring victory over sin.

We know from 2 Chronicles 17 that Jehoshaphat had one million, six hundred thousand men in his army. How, do you think, did all those soldiers feel when their king said he was powerless against the enemy? I'd say they were humiliated. Our human nature is like that vast army, proud of what it can do. But we must let go of all that pride and admit our helplessness to God. The apostle Paul once said, "When I am weak, then I am strong" (2 Cor. 12:10). That's what Jehoshaphat was counting on here—that in his human weakness God would manifest his power.

The king also confessed, "Nor do we know what to do" (2 Chron. 20:12).

This is an amazing statement when we remember that all the citizens of Judah were listening to it. What if the President of the United States appeared on television in a time of national crisis and said, "I don't know what to do"?

The American public would take that as grounds for impeachment. Even if the President is trembling on the inside, he knows he must not show it. He must come across as a wise leader who is prepared for any situation.

But Jehoshaphat was not out to impress his people. He was transparent before them. He confessed his uncertainty, thus asking for the Lord's guidance.

After admitting he didn't know what to do, the king closed his prayer with these words: "But our eyes are on Thee" (v. 12).

It's easy to miss this step. When our trials hit, we look at the problem itself, or we look at what it will lead to, or we look for solutions, or we look to a friend or a counselor. Some even look to astrology and the occult. But how often do we look to our Lord?

Psalm 37:5 (*Beck*) says, "Commit your ways to the LORD, trust Him, and He will act for you." That's what Jehoshaphat was doing in his hour of crisis.

He Obeyed God's Leading in Prayer

The fourteenth verse says that before the people were dismissed that day, an answer to Jehoshaphat's prayer came from heaven. The Lord spoke through a man named Jahaziel, who said:

> "Do not fear or be dismayed because of this great multitude, for the battle is not yours but God's. . . . You need not fight in this battle; station yourselves, stand and see the salvation of the LORD on your behalf, O Judah and Jerusalem" (2 Chron. 20:15, 17).

Jehoshaphat had told the Lord he didn't know what to do. Now God was giving him specific instructions. The king and his men were not to come out to the battlefield as warriors but as spectators, because the Lord was going to fight for them.

Perhaps Jehoshaphat thought to himself, "But how is God going to fight for us? I can't understand one word of this!"

Many people struggle with the problem of "how" regarding the work of salvation. They say, "I don't understand how Christ can save me from sin by dying on the cross. It seems to me that I should do something to contribute to my salvation." But that's where faith comes in. Faith rests completely in Christ.

Jehoshaphat did not require the Lord to explain *how* he was going to fight for Judah. It was enough for him that God had promised. The passage goes on to show he was willing to follow the leading God gave him in answer to his prayer.

> And when he had consulted with the people, he appointed those who sang to the LORD and those who praised Him in holy attire, as they went out before the army and said, "Give thanks to the LORD, for His lovingkindness is everlasting" (v. 21).

Instead of drawing up ranks of soldiers, Jehoshaphat appointed a choir. And they were going to march *ahead* of the army onto the battlefield. Never had anything looked so ridiculous since Joshua's priests marched around the city of Jericho and blew trumpets to make the walls fall down.

Moreover, Jehoshaphat told his choir to sing the Lord's praises *before* the battle. That took faith. If they went down in defeat, this king would be the world's laughingstock. Here was a man who was willing to go out on a limb to obey his Lord. Jehoshaphat took seriously the guidance that came in response to his prayer.

And God honored him for it. The people's praise that day unleashed power from heaven:

> And when they began singing and praising, the LORD set ambushes against the sons of Ammon, Moab, and Mount Seir, who had come against Judah; so they were routed. For the sons of Ammon and Moab rose up against the inhabitants of Mount Seir destroying them completely, and when they had finished with the inhabitants of Seir, they helped to destroy one another (vv. 22, 23).

Who were these people the Lord had placed in ambush? Some Bible commentators think they were angels. Others believe the three nations that teamed up against Judah had no united strategy. Thus, by mistake they attacked each other with the ambushes they had intended to set for Judah. In either case, the result was "they helped to destroy one another."

What do we learn from this? That we can leave our enemies with God. We don't have to fight them. Back in verse 15 the Lord had said, "The battle is not yours but God's," and here he proved it.

He Remembered to Bless God for His Answer

After the battle, Jehoshaphat and his people "assembled in the valley of Beracah, for there they blessed the LORD. Therefore they have named that place 'The Valley of Beracah' until today" (v. 26).

Beracah is a Hebrew word meaning "blessing." What looked as though it was going to be the valley of the shadow of death for Jehoshaphat became the valley of blessing. And when we commit our cause to our heavenly

Father in faith, our struggles will also lead us to the valley of blessing. Somehow, some way, we will be able to look back on them and say, "The Lord be praised."

He Claimed God's Peace that Comes from Prayer

The story concludes on this note: "So the kingdom of Jehoshaphat was at peace, for his God gave him rest on all sides" (v. 30).

Jehoshaphat was not worried that the three kingdoms might try to regroup and attack again. Nor did he fear some other enemy. Even if one should come up against him, Jehoshaphat knew the Lord would be his helper, as before. He was in perfect peace.

Philippians 4:6, 7 promises us that when we voice our prayer requests to God with an attitude of thanksgiving, his perfect peace, which passes all understanding, will guard our hearts and minds. Do you believe that? Are you willing to trust the Lord for peace? Or are you convinced that you will always be in a state of turmoil, always restless, always stressed out? A fruitful prayer life requires a trusting heart.

Personal Application

In what area of your life do you relate to King Jehoshaphat? What has you stumped, so that you don't know what to do? Is it your marriage that Satan is trying to destroy? A relationship with a friend who has turned against you? Maybe you are uncertain as to how to witness effectively to a neighbor who needs Jesus. Or perhaps you're at a total loss concerning one of your children who has rebelled against the Lord Jesus. All these problems fit within the realm of spiritual warfare. The battle is not ours but God's.

So when you feel helpless and don't know what to do, look to Christ. See him dying on the cross, and it will convince you that he cares. See him risen from the dead, and it will reassure you of his power over any enemy. See him interceding at the Father's right hand in heaven for you, and you will be encouraged to pray more fervently yourself.

God will always reward the look of faith toward his Son. If it could release the power of heaven in Jehoshaphat's life, it will bring us the power we need to make wise decisions in our times of crisis.

Lord, we don't know what to do, but our eyes are on you.

9

The Prayer Life of Nehemiah

Sending Up Heavenly Telegrams

Come with me back to the year 445 B.C. Nehemiah, a Jew who has risen to royal prominence in the Persian Empire as the official cupbearer to the king, is meditating on the history of his people over the last century and a half. The thoughts are painful. He ponders the nightmare of 586 B.C., when King Nebuchadnezzar's Babylonian army marched into the holy city of Jerusalem, destroying the sacred temple and forcing the Jews into exile.

But the Lord had his plan. Just as the prophet Jeremiah had predicted, the captivity lasted seventy years, after which the Jews were free to return home. The first matter of business once they arrived was to rebuild the temple. But from that time until Nehemiah's more than seventy years later almost nothing had been done to restore the walls of Jerusalem.

In chapter 1 of the Book of Nehemiah one of his brothers paid him a visit from Jerusalem. He reported how the Jewish people were distressed and mistreated. He told of how the walls and gates of the city had been burned to the ground.

Hearing that, Nehemiah could do only one thing—pray. When we compare the opening verses of chapters 1 and 2, we learn that his prayer continued for four months. Nehemiah was called into the king's presence to sample his wine, and his sadness for his people was written all over his face. This was dangerous, for Scripture says elsewhere that it was against the law for anyone to appear sad or upset in front of a Persian king (Esther 4:1, 2). Secular history tells us that King Artaxerxes was an unpredictable man who placed himself at the mercy of his whimsical feelings. He could have sentenced Nehemiah to death if he had been in the mood.

When the king noticed Nehemiah's sorrow, he inquired about it. The man of God admitted he was troubled over the condition of his nation's capital. The heavenly hand was controlling the king, for he asked what his faithful servant would like to do about his burden. At that point Nehemiah probably thought to himself, Is this God's open door to send me to Jerusalem? Is this the answer to my four months of prayer?

He jumped at his opportunity, asking for permission to travel to the holy city and rebuild its walls. But just before he made his request, he breathed a prayer to God, which the king did not even notice. No one knew anything about it until years later, when Nehemiah wrote of this moment: "So I prayed to the God of heaven" (Neh. 2:4).

This prayer was sandwiched between the king's question and his cupbearer's answer. It is probably the shortest prayer in the Bible. It may not have contained any words at all. It was what James Montgomery had in mind when he wrote:

> Prayer is the soul's sincere desire,
> Unuttered or expressed;
> The motion of a hidden fire
> That trembles in the breast.
>
> Prayer is the burden of a sigh,
> The falling of a tear,
> The upward glancing of an eye,
> When none but God is near.

Nehemiah's petition is one of ten references to a specific type of prayer. The others are in 4:4, 5, 9; 5:19; 6:9, 14; 13:14, 22, 29, 31. Each of these prayers is a brief cry that leaps out of Nehemiah's heart on a moment's notice. We could call them dart prayers, emergency prayers, or heavenly telegrams.

The only telegrams I've ever received are the imitation ones sent out by those phony sweepstakes companies, informing me that I've won something if I will pay a fee to receive it. But if someone should ever send me a real telegram, I will know instantly it must be important news.

I think that's the way God looks on our telegram prayers. He takes them seriously as important business. Therefore, I want to recommend them to you.

Why Should We Pray This Way?

It's always good to have reasons for the habits we practice, and here we can point to several.

It is convenient

The heavenly telegram is the most convenient form of prayer. You can pray this way at any time and in any place. It does not require you to retreat into your closet and lock the door behind you. You can send up a dart prayer in a moment, no matter where you are.

Nehemiah was involved in the most important conversation of his life. He knew he didn't have much time to talk to God. He was unable to get down on his knees. But that did not discourage him from praying anyway.

Whenever I stand behind the pulpit of our church, I know I'm engaging in spiritual warfare. The devil would like my listeners to daydream or at least not take my words seriously. I'm also aware that one of the goals of preaching, which is to change lives, is beyond the power of human strength. So while I'm speaking to my people, I'm saying to my Lord, "Help me to get through to them," or "Help them to see," or "Don't let Satan have his way! Have your way instead."

I advise you to pray that way when you are sharing Christ with a nonbeliever. Don't just bear witness. Intercede in prayer, too. Since you're doing both at the same time, your requests must be brief. But they will also be blessed.

It keeps us in continuous fellowship with Christ

You may be in an office all day, or in a school, or out on the road. But no matter how busy you are, your day can still be filled with prayer.

Talk about a busy man. While rebuilding Jerusalem's wall Nehemiah had to work with one hand and fight off enemies with a weapon in his other hand. He worked straight through for fifty-two days until the project was completed. He repeatedly said, "I am doing a great work, and I cannot come down." Yet in spite of his busy schedule, he was able to saturate the entire endeavor with prayer.

The apostle Paul told us to "pray at all times" (Eph. 6:18; 1 Thess. 5:17). This has puzzled many Christians, who wonder how this is possible. If your prayer life is so narrow that you won't speak to God unless you have a season of time in which to do it, then Paul's command is impossible. But if you make a habit of shooting dart prayers up to the Lord, you can maintain continuous fellowship with him.

It is effective

Although Nehemiah's prayer in the king's presence was merely a lifting of his eyes to heaven, it was still powerful enough that he remembered it twenty years later when he wrote his book. King Artaxerxes not only agreed to let Nehemiah leave for Jerusalem, he also gave him army officers and troops to protect him, as well as enough timber to rebuild Jerusalem's wall and construct a house for himself. He even appointed Nehemiah governor of Jerusalem.

Moreover, by granting Nehemiah's request, the king unknowingly fulfilled the first part of Daniel 9:25. This set in motion a specific time period before the coming of the Messiah. So it was through this dart prayer that a prophecy foretelling Jesus Christ was fulfilled.

When our Lord was dying on the cross, one of the thieves who was crucified next to him said, "Jesus, remember me when You come into your kingdom" (Luke 23:42). Both in English and the original Greek, that prayer was only nine words long. But it evoked this response from Christ: "Truly I say to you, today you shall be with Me in Paradise" (Luke 23:43).

So do not assume that brief prayers have no significance with God. Eternity alone will reveal how much was accomplished by the silent requests we send to heaven.

It guards against pride

Another good thing about prayer missiles is that they prevent us from showing off. Nehemiah never performed a miracle, yet he overcame enormous opposition as he served his Lord. His life may not impress us as does that of a Moses or an Elijah, but Nehemiah's prayers were just as mighty.

Jesus warned us of the temptation to place our prayers on parade. He told us not to heap up needless phrases or to pray in public places to be admired (Matt. 6:5, 7). All too often in conversational group prayer we feel the temptation to impress people with our petitions. But this pageantry of prayer is nonexistent when you send a telegram to heaven. It's so short and usually silent that other people will not notice it.

It is an antidote for sin

When a person uses God's name in vain, it is a perversion of a dart prayer. Have you ever stopped to think that when someone pronounces God's damnation on someone else, he is praying for God's judgment? We need a Christian countermeasure to check this profanity. Why not cultivate the habit of saying, "God bless you"? Especially if you used to call down God's curse on others, you would do well now that you are converted to pray for his blessings to rest on them.

Scripture speaks of how even the devil launches his "flaming missiles" against people (Eph. 6:16). So we Christians should be sending up heavenly missiles. When Satan launches a rocket of temptation against us, we can fire a rocketlike prayer to God. When someone utters a curse, we can counter it with a plea for God's blessing.

When Should We Pray This Way?

There is nothing wrong with offering a dart prayer at any time. But I think there are certain occasions when it is especially appropriate.

When we want to thank God

"Thank you, Lord!" is an arrow we should shoot up to heaven often. When I visit and pray for suffering people in the hospital, I almost always breathe another prayer of thanks to God as I walk out of the building. On several occasions I've been the patient in the room, confined to a bed. I know something of what it's like to be the sufferer. So I'm grateful when I can be the visitor, encourager, and minister.

Every time a certain man in our church takes either the bread or the cup of the Lord's Supper, I hear him quietly say, "Thank you, Jesus." He can't help himself. The next time God sends you a blessing, take a moment to say, even if it's only in your heart, "Praise the Lord!" or "Thank you, Jesus."

At the Last Supper, Jesus took the cup, representing his shed blood on the cross, and gave thanks (Matt. 26:27). I doubt if there is a greater example of thanks in Scripture. If our Lord could praise the Father for his death at Calvary, surely you and I should be able to thank him in any situation.

When we are in a trial

When you feel as if the world were caving in on you, ask God to help you. The last chapter of Nehemiah's book illustrates this. There were so many mixed marriages among his people that the children growing up could not speak Hebrew. They were conversing in a hodgepodge of languages. Even the grandson of the high priest had married into the family of Nehemiah's worst enemy, Sanballat, who had tried to overthrow the rebuilding of Jerusalem's wall. In the face of this confusion, Nehemiah shot up the arrow prayer found in chapter 13 verse 29.

We find another example of this from the life of Moses. In the fourteenth chapter of Exodus, Moses and the Israelites had just escaped from Egyptian slavery. As they left Egypt, they came up against the Red Sea, while Pharaoh and his army were closing in on them from behind. Moses and the people of Israel were in a seemingly doomed position. But by faith Moses promised that the Lord would fight for them. In verse 15 God asked Moses, "Why are you crying out to Me?"

Oddly, there is no record of Moses crying out to God. He had been talking to the Hebrews, not to the Lord—or so it seemed. The point is that while Moses spoke to the people he was also praying in his heart. And God granted his prayer by parting the Red Sea. This was another dart prayer not recorded in words. Maybe it contained none. It may have been only a frightened glance up to heaven, as if to ask for help. No one knew anything about Moses' prayer on this occasion. Yet God performed a miracle in answer to it.

Maybe your life is a shambles right now. When you feel the chaos threatening from all sides, take a deep breath and let out a prayer to your Lord. When the housework is endless and the children mess up their rooms faster than you can clean them, send a wire to God, pleading for help. When the checkbook won't balance and the bills are backing up on you, don't be so frantic that you can't lift up a prayer. When someone is getting on your nerves and you're ready to explode in anger, quickly ask the Lord to help you keep your cool. He is a God of order, so we should and can go to him when our lives are in disorder.

When danger threatens

In Nehemiah's fourth chapter, a mob riot nearly broke out, because his enemies did not like the progress he was making on the wall. As he recounted the danger he was in, Nehemiah wrote: "But we prayed to our God" (Neh. 4:9).

To take another example, think back to when Jesus' disciples were caught in a storm at sea in the middle of the night. They rushed over to Jesus, awakened him, and cried out, "Save us Lord; we are perishing!" (Matt. 8:25). Jesus stood up, rebuked the wind and waves, and there was perfect calm.

Again, recall when Peter was walking on the water toward Christ. After the waves slapped him in the face a few times, he began to sink. But as he was going down, he called out three words: "Lord, save me!" (Matt. 14:30). And in the next instant Jesus rescued him from a watery grave.

Years ago I was driving toward an intersection where the light was yellow. I had one of those tough decisions to make: whether to throw on the brakes or try to make it through the light. Another car was heading toward the same intersection at a ninety degree angle to me. Its driver could see that her light was about to turn green, so she did not slow down. The result was that I was in the intersection when the light turned red, and she was entering it at the moment it turned green for her. She hit the rear fender of my car. I had three passengers with me and was terribly embarrassed. I pulled over to the side of the road, and before we stepped out of the car, I pitched up a dart prayer to God. I remember saying something like this: "Lord, thanks that we're not hurt, and please let the people in the other car be free from injury, too."

God more than answered that prayer. Not only were the two women in the other car unhurt, but the policeman who witnessed the accident issued neither me nor the other driver a ticket. To top it all off, because we were both insured by the same company neither one of us had to pay a deductible on the claim.

When we are in an emergency

In some situations a heavenly telegram is the only way we *can* pray, because we have so little time. A friend of mine, nearly sixty years old, once fell about ten feet from a tree in his backyard. He later told me that in that instant before he hit the ground he prayed, "God, help me!" And sure enough, he was uninjured.

In your moments of desperation, lift your spirit up to God. Your prayer can reach heaven and back before the crisis hits!

When we are discouraged

There were two occasions in the story of Nehemiah when discouragement threatened him. In chapter 4 of the book, his enemies ridiculed the builders, accusing them of using charred stones. They laughed and said that if even a fox would walk on their newly constructed wall, it would collapse. Then in verses 4 and 5 Nehemiah shot up an arrow prayer. In it he admitted to God that the builders had been demoralized. But in answer to his prayer the heavenly Father gave them fresh strength to persevere.

In the sixth chapter, Sanballat sent a servant to slander

Nehemiah in front of the other workers. He concocted a story about Nehemiah wanting to overthrow the government and become a king. Our friend answered that he knew his enemies were only trying to discourage the laborers and abort the work. Then he prayed, "But now, O God, strengthen my hands" (Neh. 6:9).

Nehemiah's prayer in Hebrew is only four words long, yet God did strengthen his hands and save him and his men from discouragement. In the Living Bible the prayer is placed in parentheses. The Holy Spirit wants us to see that we can pray under our breath whenever depression hits.

What threatens to sink your spirits today? Maybe you're already discouraged. Have you prayed about it, even with a brief, heavenly telegram? If you feel like quitting, admit that and ask God to strengthen you against it. If Nehemiah had given up, the Jerusalem wall would have remained in ruins, the Jewish people would not have been revived, and the book telling of his great victory would never have been penned.

Think how much you have to lose by throwing in the towel when God has told you to persevere. You owe it to him to pray before you let discouragement devour you.

Personal Application

I see four simple lessons that stand out from Nehemiah's prayer life. First, his holy telegrams teach us that God cares very much about even our faintest prayers. Second, we learn that the heavenly Father not only loves to hear our quick cries but also loves to answer them. Third, we discover that even the little prayers concerning small things bring about gigantic results. Who knows what wonders the Lord is accomplishing right now in answer to the heavenly telegrams we send up for ourselves and others?

And finally, Nehemiah shows us that dart prayers supplement a healthy prayer life. This was not his only method of prayer; I remind you of Nehemiah's four-month prayer reported in chapter 1 of his book. We may compare dart prayers to between-meal snacks. They satisfy us for the time being and fulfill a need, but we would not want to live on them alone.

Still, however, cultivate the habit of sending telegram prayers. Though brief, they are welcomed by God as a genuine article of prayer.

10

The Prayer Life of David
Unconditional Surrender to God

No one has more of his prayers recorded in the Bible than King David of Israel. Most of the psalms he penned are personal conversations with his Lord. His life's story is told in the Books of 1 and 2 Samuel and 1 Chronicles; and there, too, David proves to be a man with a deep spiritual life.

It would be an enormous task to examine every single prayer of David, so we shall look at three representative examples. Each one illustrates his habit of showing unconditional surrender to God.

David's Unpleasant Prayer for His Sin

Though David is described as a man after God's own heart (1 Sam. 13:14), he fell into notorious sin. In a moment of weakness he committed adultery with Bathsheba. And after she became pregnant by him, David felt compelled to mastermind the death of her husband, who was serving in the army. From all outward appearances Uriah perished on the battlefield as a war casualty, but David was responsible. And once Uriah was out of the way, the scheming king married Bathsheba.

Of course none of this pleased God, who directed the prophet Nathan to confront David for his sins of adultery and murder. Psalm 51 is the result. In it David pours out his repentant heart to the Lord in a plea for pardon. Here he surrenders his sins to God. He cries, "Wash me thoroughly from my iniquity, and cleanse me from my sin" (Ps. 51:2).

David begs not for the removal of the punishment of his sin but of the sin itself. He hates what he did. He begs the Lord to scrub him thoroughly from his iniquity. He uses two words, *wash* and *cleanse*. Perhaps he means, "If water cannot wash my sin away, then cleanse me with fire—anything that will make me pure."

He goes on to say, "Thou art . . . blameless when Thou dost judge" (Ps. 51:4).

David is confessing that his sins deserve the strictest punishment. If God had sent him to hell, David would have replied, "Yes, Lord; that is fair." He knows there is no excuse for sin, so he does not offer any.

He continues, "Behold, I was brought forth in iniquity; and in sin my mother conceived me" (Ps. 51:5).

By this David means, "It's not just that I committed sin, but that I am sin. It's the raw material of my human nature."

While confessing your sin to God, have you ever said, "Lord, that wasn't like me to rebel against you; I don't know what got into me"? People who say that don't understand themselves. It *is* like us to betray God, because sin got into us at the moment of conception. Scripture compares us to sheep whose nature is to go astray (Isa. 53:6). In his hymn "Come, Thou Fount of Every Blessing" Robert Robinson put it this way:

> Prone to wander, Lord, I feel it;
> Prone to leave the God I love.

Do you feel that tendency? Even we who love Jesus are inclined to forsake him. Though we are new creatures in Christ, the old nature lives on inside us. David understood that.

Here is something else he sensed: "Thou dost desire truth in the innermost being" (Ps. 51:6). And what God desired, David had not produced. He had been dealing in deception for nine months before Nathan exposed him. However, it was not only truth on his lips that God was looking for but truth "in the innermost being." The Lord wanted to see more than a superficial change in David. And in this prayer of confession David yearns for that, too.

The following verse shows us that the best prayers of confession also include faith: "Wash me, and I shall be whiter than snow" (Ps. 51:7).

Judas Iscariot made a humble confession when he said, "I have sinned by betraying innocent blood" (Matt. 27:4). But the very next verse tells us he hanged himself. He could not trust Christ for forgiveness, and that cost him his soul.

David, however, even through tears of deepest spiritual pain, has faith that he "shall be whiter than snow." That reminds us of what God promised in Isaiah 1:18, "Though your sins are as scarlet, they will be as white as snow."

Have you ever said to yourself, "I believe the Lord will forgive others, but not me"? That may sound humble, but such unbelief insults the blood of Christ.

In Psalm 51:10 this great man of prayer makes another bold request: "Create in me a clean heart, O God."

The word *create* implies that sin is a destroyer. It does so much damage that even almighty God cannot restore it. He has to crucify the old heart and create a brand-new one from scratch. The heavenly Father is not interested in *re*forming us; he knows we need *trans*forming.

David has lusted with his eyes for Bathsheba. But he does not ask God to give him better eyes. Instead, he pleads for a clean heart. If you tell lies, your trouble is not on your tongue; it's in your heart. If you devour every morsel of gossip you hear about other people, the problem is not in your ears; it's in your heart. Maybe you crave food and are a glutton; or possibly ingesting one drop of alcohol will cause you to lose control and become drunk. There is nothing wrong with your taste buds; the problem lies much deeper. Gang members use guns and knives, not because their hands are murderous but because their hearts are.

David went to the core of his problem when he prayed, "Create in me a clean heart, O God." He begged for a cure that would change him from the inside out.

He also pleaded, "Restore to me the joy of Thy salvation" (Ps. 51:12).

We think happiness is found in sinful pleasures, but David's example teaches us that they only make us miserable. When David invited Bathsheba into his bedroom, the Lord departed and took the joy of David's salvation with him.

David understood that through his sin he did not lose his salvation; he lost the joy of it. But that was no trifle to this man. Sometimes when I've confronted believers with their sin, they have said, "I'm not worried about it. All I'm losing is my fellowship with God, not my relationship." But is that a small matter? If it is to you, you have good reason to question the authenticity of your conversion. Fellowship with Christ produces life's sweetest joy, and the loss of it yields the bitterest sorrow.

David's request for renewed joy comes only after a thorough confession of his sin and corruption. Many people try to reverse the order. They beg God, "Please let me be happy. Take away my misery." But they have not first asked him to remove the sins that have caused their misery. Happiness is never found in a direct pursuit. It comes as a by-product of being right with God because Jesus is our Savior from sin.

In verse 13 David binds himself to a promise: "Then I will teach transgressors Thy ways, and sinners will be converted to Thee."

He is saying, "If only you will forgive me, Lord, I'll bring other sinners like myself to you." Of course we should not bargain with the heavenly Father. People who do seldom keep their end of the agreement, anyway. But I don't think David is trying to strike a deal with God. Instead, he is saying, "Lord, I know your forgiveness is not meant for me alone, but also for others. I will commit myself to teaching them your ways and leading them to you." Not only did David do that in life, but even in death this psalm he wrote still shows us God's ways of forgiveness and love.

Next David prays, "Deliver me from bloodguiltiness, O God" (Ps. 51:14).

When David first heard of Uriah's death in battle, he justified it with these words: "Do not let this thing displease you, for the sword devours one as well as another"

(2 Sam. 11:25). He was shrugging his shoulders and saying, "That's the way it goes in war. You never know who's going to die."

But David did know. He had orchestrated Uriah's death by having him placed in the front line of the fiercest battle and ordering the rest of the army to forsake him (2 Sam. 11:15). Now he calls his act by its rightful name: bloodguiltiness. Uriah's blood was on David's hands.

In 1859 the American Medical Association labeled abortion "wanton and murderous destruction." By 1967 it had become "the interruption of an unwanted pregnancy." And now many people call it "a medical procedure." Those who are committing adultery would say they are having an affair or a meaningful relationship. It's in vogue to speak of the perversion of homosexuality as an acceptable alternative lifestyle.

But these whitewashes do not impress God. Abraham Lincoln once asked a critic, "How many legs would a cow have if you counted its tail as a leg?"

"Five," was the answer.

"No," said Lincoln. "Just calling a tail a leg doesn't make it a leg."

We can call our sin by some other name, but that does not make it right. David came face to face with the ugliness of his sin, and so must we if we expect to receive God's forgiveness.

David's Unsuccessful Prayer for His Son

After David's prayer of confession in Psalm 51, "the LORD struck the child that Uriah's widow bore to David, so that he was very sick" (2 Sam. 12:15).

That surprises us, especially after David's heartfelt repentance and cries for forgiveness.

David therefore inquired of God for the child; and David
fasted and went and lay all night on the ground. And the
elders of his household stood beside him in order to raise
him up from the ground, but he was unwilling and would
not eat food with them. Then it happened on the seventh
day that the child died (2 Sam. 12:16–18).

If ever there was a man who knew how to pray, it was
David. The Book of Psalms proves that. He also fasted and
prostrated himself on the ground for a week. We can only
begin to imagine the intensity of this prayer. I can hear
David cry, "Take me, if you have to, Lord, but not this
child. I'm the one who sinned. He has done nothing wrong.
O God, no! Please, no!" The request, however, was denied.

But when David saw that his servants were whispering
together, David perceived that the child was dead; so
David said to his servants, "Is the child dead?" And they
said, "He is dead" (2 Sam. 12:19).

How would you have responded to that news? Maybe
you have lost a child in death. Or you may be a widow
who has seen two or three husbands die from cancer. I've
counseled some people in those situations who are angry
and bitter toward God. They accuse him of cruelty and
refuse to love or serve him in the future.

See how David responded: "So David arose from the
ground, washed, anointed himself, and changed his
clothes; and he came into the house of the LORD and worshiped" (2 Sam. 12:20).

In his prayer of confession, David had said, "Thou art
. . . blameless when Thou dost judge" (Ps. 51:4). And now
he proves it by worshiping the Lord after the death of his
son. To many people, worship is bowing in prayer, singing
a few hymns, and listening to a sermon. But it is possible

to do all those things and still have your heart far from Christ. The Bible compares us to sheep, servants, clay, and children. Worship, then, is the sheep following the shepherd, the servants bowing before their master, the clay being soft enough so the potter can mold it, and the children loving their heavenly Father more than anyone or anything else. To put it in one word, worship is *surrender*. In this prayer David surrendered his son to God.

So did Abraham. Therefore he obeyed without hesitation when the Lord told him to offer Isaac on the altar of sacrifice. Job, too, remained faithful when his ten children died in a hurricane. After hearing the news, he said, "The LORD gave and the LORD has taken away. Blessed be the name of the LORD" (Job 1:21). Abraham and Job, like David, knew how to worship.

Do you? Without heart-rooted worship that bows even to God's mysterious ways, there is no true prayer. The character of our faith is most tested when God denies our pleas. Without a willingness to surrender our nearest and dearest to the Lord, our prayers are a sham.

David's Unceasing Prayer for His Savior

The one word that is found on David's lips in prayer more than any other is *praise*. In the Book of Psalms it occurs 166 times. Here are just a few examples, all from psalms that David wrote: "His praise shall continually be in my mouth" (34:1). "My tongue shall declare . . . Thy praise all day long" (35:28). "Because Thy lovingkindness is better than life, my lips will praise Thee" (63:3). "I will sing praise to my God while I have my being" (104:33). "Seven times a day I praise Thee" (119:164).

Praise is an unconditional expression of worship, love, and thanks to God.

While I was a college student, I invested two of my summers counseling high school students at Mount Hermon Christian Conference Center in California. They had a two-man volleyball court there, and each week I'd team up with one of the guys in my cabin. I remember one who had the habit of saying, "Praise the Lord!" whenever we won a point. But if we lost the point, he said something that bordered on profanity. I took the opportunity to explain to him that his praise was conditioned on our winning a point in a meaningless game, and that nullified its value. Conditional praise is not praise at all; it is selfish ambition.

David spent years running for his life from the wicked King Saul. His favorite wife was taken away from him. He suffered through the rebellion of his own sons. He agonized under the disciplining hand of God. Yet his prayers continued to sing with the chorus of praise.

On May 21, 1738, Charles Wesley trusted Jesus Christ for his salvation. That same afternoon he wrote these words of praise:

> Where shall my wondering soul begin?
> How shall I all to heaven aspire?
> A slave redeemed from death and sin,
> A brand plucked from eternal fire,
> How shall I equal triumphs raise,
> Or sing my great Deliverer's praise?

Each year until his death fifty years later Charles Wesley composed a hymn of praise to Christ on his Christian birthday. Just before the first anniversary of his spiritual change, Wesley told a friend, Peter Boehler, about his joy in Christ. Then he added, "But I suppose I should keep quiet about it."

Boehler replied, "If I had a thousand tongues, I would use them all to praise the Lord Jesus!"

Challenged by his friend's words, Charles Wesley sat down on the first anniversary of his conversion and wrote this hymn that has thrived through the centuries:

> O for a thousand tongues to sing
> My great Redeemer's praise,
> The glories of my God and King,
> The triumphs of His grace.

Of course God has not given each of us a thousand tongues with which to praise him, but he has given one. Are you using yours to sing God's praise unconditionally? The opposite is to use your tongue to curse, lie, grumble, and gossip.

When David praised his Lord, he was pouring out an unconditional surrender of his heart. This was the unceasing prayer of his life.

Personal Application

We have summed up David's prayer life by studying three representative prayers. Does your prayer life include these three kinds of petitions?

First, confession; when was the last time you confessed your sins to the heavenly Father? Surely this is something you need to do every day. Have you been taking God's forgiveness for granted lately? What specific sin is the Holy Spirit convicting you of? Confession makes for unpleasant prayers, because it exposes our rottenness. But until we bring our sins to the surface, God will not wash them away.

Second, have you been making an unsuccessful prayer to God lately? Maybe you've begged the heavenly Father for a certain marriage partner or a particular job opening, but he has denied you. You asked the Lord for a definite answer to prayer, but he said no. Countless times in the nearly twenty-five years since I was stricken with diabetes, I've prayed for healing. But instead God has sustained me with his all-sufficient grace.

Every Christian sends up prayers that miss the mark. We should be ashamed only if we respond negatively to God's refusals. David was able to worship, even after the Lord denied his plea to spare his innocent son. It sounds strange, even cruel to us. But that's where faith means so much. The baby's death reminds us that God owes us not even one week of life.

Third, is there praise in your prayers? Whether David's heart was filled with rapture or broken with sorrow, this was the theme of his unceasing prayer. Some Christians feel odd saying, "Praise the Lord!" They think it has become hackneyed by the many who have overused it. Still, it is a scriptural phrase, and we would do well to utter it. Most of all, let's make sure we live it.

Confession of sin, worship of God when he deprives us of our hearts' desire, and continuous praise are marks of the prayer life of a believer who practices unconditional surrender to his Lord. This is what made David a man after God's own heart. He was the kind of believer all God's children want to be, and can be.

11

The Prayer Life of Daniel
Securing Deliverance from Death

In the twelve chapters of the Book of Daniel, we hear the prophet appealing to God in prayer at three prominent stages in his life. In each one he secured deliverance from death. The most famous example is the episode of Daniel in the lions' den. There his prayers saved him from a grisly slaughter. Before that, the prophet's petitions rescued the wise men of Babylon from execution. And later in his life Daniel pleaded that Israel would be delivered from a well-deserved curse brought on by their defiance of the Lord.

All three pleas for deliverance were granted. Through Daniel's petitions he himself, the pagan wise men of Babylon, and God's own people were spared from judgment. Daniel's three prayers reveal six principles we should practice.

Daniel's Prayer for Interpretation

In the second chapter of the Book of Daniel, King Nebuchadnezzar was frightened by a nightmare and asked his wise men to tell him two things: the content and the interpretation of his dream. When they confessed their inability to do either, the king sentenced them to death. Daniel and his three Jewish friends were among those wise men, though Nebuchadnezzar had not bothered to ask them for understanding. And when Daniel learned of the imminent execution, he

> went in and requested of the king that he would give him time, in order that he might declare the interpretation to the king. Then Daniel went to his house and informed his friends, Hananiah, Mishael and Azariah, about the matter, in order that they might request compassion from the God of heaven concerning this mystery, so that Daniel and his friends might not be destroyed with the rest of the wise men of Babylon (Dan. 2:16–18).

He prayed as a first resort

Perhaps Daniel, on hearing the news of his death sentence, was tempted to say, "This is no time to pray; I've got to do something—fast!" He could have called all his fellow wise men together and mapped out a strategy of defense. They might even have planned to assassinate the deranged king before he could execute them. At the very least Daniel might have debated with Nebuchadnezzar as to why he should not carry out his order. The prophet marched into the king's court, all right. But all he asked for was time to pray. That was his first resort.

Daniel knew that God had singled him out in the Babylonian kingdom for such a time as this. But he never presumed that the Lord would reveal Nebuchadnezzar's dream and its interpretation without the need for prayer. He believed that fulfilling God's plan for his life was a reason why he *should* pray, not an excuse for neglecting it.

The request itself was a tall one. Daniel needed to know the content and interpretation of Nebuchadnezzar's dream. Even the king himself could not remember his nightmare. Daniel might have despaired and said, "Who does the king think I am? I can't read his mind. I can't look into a crystal ball. This is hopeless." But he was confident that there was "a God in heaven who reveals mysteries" (Dan. 2:27). Daniel's only lead in solving this mystery was the Lord. That was enough for him. He was content to have prayer as his only resort.

He prayed in fellowship with other believers

Daniel did not pray solo. He immediately appealed to his three friends, Hananiah, Mishael, and Azariah, to pray with him. (We know them better by their Babylonian names: Shadrach, Meshach, and Abednego.) More than social friends, they were his prayer partners.

Do you have a prayer partner? When temptation hits you right between the eyes, can you confide in someone who will intercede for you? Is anyone else pleading with you at God's throne of grace for the salvation of people you love? Do you and your spouse regularly bow together before the Lord? And do you include your children? Are you a family of prayer?

Daniel ranks as one of the greatest heroes in the Bible. Yet even he did not dare pray alone if he could help it. How much more do you and I need prayer partners! Surely we require all the help we can marshal when engaged in spiritual warfare. Jesus said that he is present wherever two or three believers gather in his name (Matt. 18:20). Thus he encourages us to pray together.

The evening that Daniel and his three friends laid out their petition before God, "the mystery was revealed to Daniel in a night vision" (Dan. 2:19).

Perhaps God repeated Nebuchadnezzar's dream for Daniel while he slept. This was one rerun worth watching. Though four men had prayed, only one received the answer. But were the other three jealous? No! Prayer partners sense a unity with each other. It makes no difference to them who receives the answer to prayer, as long as it comes. When Daniel received his wisdom from God, it secured deliverance from certain death for Babylon's wise men.

Daniel's Prayer for Intervention

The second example of Daniel in prayer centers around his well-known encounter with the lions. Darius the Mede was in power, and Daniel was nearly ninety years old. God had distinguished him in the kingdom, and that aroused the jealousy of Daniel's fellow rulers. When they were unable to discover grounds for reproach in him, they devised a fail-safe scheme to trip him up. They wrote a law that prohibited prayer for thirty days to anyone but King Darius. The law, however, was a farce, because the lawmakers designed it to be violated. Daniel 6:10 tells us of his response:

> Now when Daniel knew that the document was signed, he entered his house (now in his roof chamber he had windows open toward Jerusalem); and he continued kneeling on his knees three times a day, praying and giving thanks before his God, as he had been doing previously.

He prayed regularly

Daniel was "on his knees three times a day," probably morning, noon, and night. Prayer was not something he did haphazardly or only when an emergency struck. It was a practice he refused to discontinue. He was consistent in his spiritual disciplines.

David testified in Psalm 119:164, "Seven times a day I praise Thee." The Levites were responsible to "stand every morning to thank and to praise the Lord, and likewise at evening" (1 Chron. 23:30). And in the New Testament we read that three o'clock in the afternoon was set apart as "the hour of prayer" (Acts 3:1).

When are your regular times to be alone with God? Experience has taught me that if I don't schedule a time, I won't find it. The trouble with planning to give the Lord our leftover time is that there usually is none left over. If we don't pray regularly, we don't pray at all.

He prayed steadfastly

King Darius had a policy that once he signed a law there was no revoking it. But Daniel had a policy of his own. Even when threatened with the most gruesome form of capital punishment, he refused to back down from time alone with his Lord.

Our hero might have compromised in several ways. He could have taken a month's leave of absence from his personal altar. Or he might have prayed after dark when no one would be able to see him. Or he could have prayed silently; the Lord can hear his children even when their knees are unbowed and their lips unmoving. That would have outfoxed the conspirators.

But Daniel would have none of this. For him the issue was not life or death but unashamed loyalty to his Lord. It was not as though he threw open his windows in defiance of the law. The text implies that his windows were already open, and he refused to close them. Nor was Daniel showing off when he prayed. In those days windows were built small to protect against the heat, and high as a defense against thieves. Consequently, he could be seen only by people willing to go out of their way to spy on him.

What if our government outlawed prayer for a month, not as a misdemeanor but as a capital offense? Would you, like Daniel, remain steadfast? Such an edict wouldn't affect some professing Christians in the slightest. In their daily experience they've already outlawed prayer. You may think I'm exaggerating, but I've noticed that some believers don't even pause to thank God for their food on the table. And that makes me wonder, If they don't say a simple grace, will they take time out for longer prayers?

Daniel found it impossible to cease praying for two reasons. First, he loved the Lord too much. Second, he had formed a habit over the years that even the law could not break. Perhaps right now your prayer life is erratic. You mumble a few words to God at bedtime, but the next night you don't even do that, nor the following night. Maybe you go for a week or two without any conversation with the Lord.

That can change. It takes personal discipline, but you can form good habits of prayer. A habit is like a cable that's made up of many threads. Each thread could be one day's quiet time with God. Every day a new strand is intertwined with the others. And in a few months you're forming a cable that won't be broken. You're learning steadfastness in prayer.

Your lions' den might be a prayerless life. But just like Daniel, you can be delivered from it.

Daniel's Prayer of Intercession

In the ninth chapter of this prophetic book we read Daniel's longest recorded prayer. He intercedes for the Jews, who had been living in exile for more than a generation. This prayer presents us with two more characteristics of a believer who secures deliverance from death.

He prayed in response to Scripture

> In the first year of Darius . . . I, Daniel, observed in the books the number of the years which was revealed as the word of the LORD to Jeremiah the prophet for the completion of the desolations of Jerusalem, namely, seventy years. So I gave my attention to the LORD God to seek Him by prayer and supplications. (Dan. 9:1–3).

Daniel was a prophet, yet even he felt the need to study the books of Scripture. How much more do you and I have the same need! While reading the Book of Jeremiah, Daniel learned that his people would remain in captivity for seventy years. In Jeremiah 29:10 he found this promise: "For thus says the LORD, 'When seventy years have been completed for Babylon, I will visit you and fulfill My good word to you, to bring you back to this place.'"

Daniel further testifies that he found this promise "in the first year of Darius," which was 537 B.C. The invasion of Jerusalem began in 605 B.C., sixty-eight years earlier. So there remained only two more years before the Jews would be free to return to their holy city.

When he learned that, Daniel prayed for the fulfillment of God's promise. He might have said, "A promise is a promise, and therefore it will surely happen. So I don't have to pray." But his faith was more practical than that. For him, the promise was a reason why he could ask God to bring it about.

Many people have merely a speculative interest in prophecy. They see signs of Christ's second coming in every current event. Others delight in arguing over when Jesus will return. But when John received the prophecy of Christ's return and recorded it in the Book of Revelation, he prayed, "Amen. Come, Lord Jesus" (Rev. 22:20). For Daniel and John, the prophetic promises were grounds for prayer. And their examples teach us to pray in response to what we read in the Bible.

Let me illustrate. Jesus told us in Matthew 9:38 to "beseech the Lord of the harvest to send out workers into His harvest." You've read that many times. But have you ever stopped right there and acted on your Lord's command? Have you ever prayed, "Heavenly Father, move in people's hearts all over the world to become witnesses, missionaries, evangelists, and pastors who will reap a great harvest for Christ"?

When you read in the Bible of hard-hearted Pharaoh, jealous Saul, adulterous David, self-righteous Pharisees, doubting Thomas, or traitorous Judas, do you say, "How could they do those things?" Such a response misses the intention of God in Scripture. Instead of criticizing the biblical villains, our Lord wants us to see ourselves in them and pray for forgiveness.

When you read of Jesus making blind men see, pray that he will open the eyes of people you know who don't see the truth of the gospel. When Scripture commands you to share your faith, pray for courage and wisdom. When you read of biblical people who were filled with the Spirit, ask the heavenly Father to fill you. When the Bible tells you not to worry, say, "Jesus, I cast my cares on you." Daniel prayed about what he read in Scripture, and so should we.

He identified with others in his prayers

Every time I read this ninth chapter of Daniel, I find the prophet's confession of sin striking. Of course he was not perfect, and he required a Savior. But no flaw of his is mentioned in Scripture. His name occurs a total of seventy-eight times in three biblical books, and his story extends from his youth into his old age. Yet we cannot pinpoint one specific sin. Even faultfinders who hated him could discover no blemish on his record (Dan. 6:4). So in his prayer of confession, we expect him to say, "O Lord, forgive these stiff-necked people. They have acted wickedly. They have transgressed your laws." But no, he includes himself in a confession of flagrant sin. He says:

> "We have sinned, committed iniquity, acted wickedly, and rebelled, even turning aside from Thy commandments and ordinances. Moreover, we have not listened to Thy servants the prophets " (Dan. 9:5, 6).

He voices six confessions, each with a different meaning. We can paraphrase them as follows: "Lord, we have fallen short of your standard. We have forsaken the right course. Our conduct has been wicked. Our hearts have been rebellious. We have defied your laws. And we have scorned your servants, the prophets." That last confession is remarkable when we recall that Daniel was one of the prophets. We could expect him to say, "Lord, these people have scorned me." But he identifies himself with the scorners, not the prophets.

He continues:

> "Righteousness belongs to Thee, O Lord, but to us open shame. . . . Open shame belongs to us, O Lord . . . because we have sinned against Thee. . . . We have rebelled . . . nor

They Knew How to Pray

have we obeyed the voice of the LORD our God. . . . So the
curse has been poured out on us . . . for we have sinned.
. . . We have not sought the favor of the LORD our God by
turning from our iniquity and giving attention to Thy
truth. . . . We have not obeyed. . . . We have sinned, we
have been wicked" (Dan. 9:7–11, 13–15).

There is no self-righteousness there. Daniel uses the
pronouns *we, us,* and *our* fourteen times. Jesus told about
a Pharisee who prayed, "God, I thank Thee that I am not
like other people: swindlers, unjust, adulterers, or even
like this tax-gatherer" (Luke 18:11). But Daniel virtually
confessed, "God, I am guilty of the same sins my people
have committed." He identified with them. Their problems were his problems.

Years ago a man who attended our church was arrested
for a serious crime. When I learned of it, I visited in his
home to pray with him and encourage him. In our discus-
sion his wife kept saying, "We have failed. We are so
ashamed. Can you ever forgive us?" This wife had no part
in the actual crime and led an exemplary Christian life.
But she identified fully with her husband. And after listening to her that afternoon, I gained new insight into the
verse that says, "The two will become one flesh. So they
are no longer two, but one" (Mark 10:8 NIV).

Daniel was "one flesh" with his people. He did not possess an us/them mentality. His inclusion of himself in his
people's sins proved his love for them.

It also made him a type of Christ. When Jesus mounted
the cross at Calvary, he did more than die for our sins. He
actually became our sins. Second Corinthians 5:21 teaches
that the heavenly Father "made Him who knew no sin to
be sin on our behalf, that we might become the righteousness of God in Him." And 1 Peter 2:24 says, "He Himself

bore our sins in His body on the cross." That's how much
Jesus identifies with us. Could there be any greater proof
of his love?

If you want to capture the heart of Daniel and the heart
of Christ himself, identify with others when you pray.
Abortion, drugs, pornography, homosexuality, and defiance of God are not America's sins; they are our sins. We
have all contributed to the guilt of our nation, at least by
failing to cry out against these crimes and by exposing our
families to them on our television sets. Yes, our own com-
placency condemns us. This is why we must identify with
the foremost of sinners in our prayers. But more than that,
love will compel us to identify with them.

Personal Application

Daniel's prayers secured deliverance from death for the
pagan wise men of Babylon, the Jewish nation, and himself. What kind of deliverance do you need? And what
about the people around you? One person requires freedom from an addictive habit, such as smoking, alcohol, or
some other drug. Another needs to be rescued from an
uncontrollable temper that is destroying his or her family.
Others are enslaved to lust, hatred, jealousy, and marital
unfaithfulness. Perhaps you require liberty from spiritual
slothfulness; you lack discipline in prayer, Bible study, and
church worship. And if you've never trusted Jesus Christ
as your personal Savior, you need to be delivered not only
from bad habits but also from a sinful nature.

To secure God's deliverance, pray Daniel's way: as a first
resort, in fellowship with other believers, regularly, stead-
fastly, in response to what you read in Scripture, and iden-
tifying with the needs, hurts, and problems of others.

12

The Prayer Life of Jonah

*Crying Out to God
from Deep Trouble*

Sooner or later every one of us sinks into the pit of trouble. You may be in the midst of an ugly divorce. Or possibly you have recently been told you have an inoperable, cancerous tumor somewhere in your body.

Maybe your teenager is involved in premarital sex. You worry that he or she might even get AIDS. Perhaps a child is an alcoholic or a drug addict. As you watch a son throw away his life you feel as if he's throwing away yours, too.

Possibly your marriage is full of trouble. Your spouse no longer loves you, and there's not a thing you can do about it. You want to rescue the relationship, but it's quickly slipping out of your grasp.

The prophet Jonah knew all about trouble. God called

him to travel east to preach in the city of Nineveh, but that was the last thing he wanted to do. So he boarded a ship headed west for Tarshish. Out at sea the Lord made Jonah pay the price for his disobedience. A fierce storm hit the ship and would not let up until the prophet convinced the sailors to toss him overboard. For the next three days he was buried alive in the stomach of a great fish. We can scarcely imagine how terrifying that was for Jonah.

Chapter 2 of the Book of Jonah records his crying out to God. Here we find nine characteristics that reveal the strength of Jonah's prayer life.

He Prayed Personally

The first verse in Jonah 2 says, "Then Jonah prayed to the LORD his God from the stomach of the fish."

Note the word *then* at the beginning of the verse. It was when he found himself inside a monstrous fish that Jonah began to speak to the Lord. Talk about being "down in the mouth"! Jonah was lower than that. In verse 2 he calls the belly of the fish "the depth of *Sheol*." And yet even from there Jonah cried out to God.

Have you ever been so depressed that you felt unable to pray? I have. Or if in imminent danger we are prone to say, "This is no time for prayer, I've got to *do* something fast!" But Jonah appealed to God from his dire circumstances. And this was no memorized petition to a supreme being. The text says he prayed "to the LORD his God." That's personal prayer.

Do you have a personal God? Can you say, "My Lord Jesus"? When a crisis hits, then you discover just how personal is your relationship with Christ. And if you learn that you've neglected the personal relationship, the crisis has served a valuable purpose.

He Prayed Fervently

In verse 2 Jonah further testifies, "I called out . . . to the LORD, . . . I cried for help."

Too often we expect a million-dollar answer to a ten-cent prayer. A lukewarm prayer is as much a contradiction in terms as a lukewarm fire. Both should burn. If our prayers are going to reach God's heart, they must first come from ours.

The ship's captain had called on Jonah to pray, lest everyone perish in the storm. But all the prophet could do was sleep. He had been running away from God. Now here he was running to him—in prayer. He was no longer sleeping, but seeking.

Which are we doing? Leonard Ravenhill writes:

> We have many organizers, but few agonizers; many players and payers, few pray-ers; many singers, few clingers; lots of pastors, few wrestlers; many fears, few tears; much fashion, little passion; many interferers, few intercessors; many writers, but few fighters. Failing here, we fail everywhere (Leonard Ravenhill, *Why Revival Tarries* [Minneapolis: Bethany Fellowship, 1979], p. 23).

Like Jonah, we need to wake up.

He Prayed in Faith

In verse 2 Jonah tells us that in the fish's stomach he "cried for help."

Imagine yourself passing through the sea monster's mouth and into its stomach. Would you think of praying at a time like that? Maybe just to say, "Lord, here I come!" but that's about it. Jonah, however, cried out for help. He was trusting God to deliver him from his plight. And that took faith.

144   They Knew How to Pray

A man needed $307 to pay his bills and had no idea
where he could come up with the money. At his wit's end
and as a last resort, he asked God in prayer to meet his
need. That afternoon the mailman delivered a tax refund
check from the IRS for exactly $307. When the man saw
it, he lifted up his eyes and said, "Lord, remember that
prayer request of mine for $307? Never mind. The prob-
lem solved itself."

He had no faith. But are we any better? Sometimes we
get down on our knees, make a request, reverently claim
the biblical promise, thank God in advance for granting it,
and then are positive it will never be ours. Scripture says
that that kind of double-minded person cannot expect to
receive anything from the Lord (James 1:7, 8). God honors faith in our prayers. Jonah believed, even when his
case looked hopeless!

He Prayed Biblically

There are eighteen parallels between Jonah's prayer and
the psalms. And he quotes fifteen different psalms. Jonah
was in the fish, but the Bible was in him.

The psalms constituted the devotional prayer book for
ancient Israel. Do you know that they can serve as a
tremendous aid to our prayers today? When you are deep
in a trial and pouring your heart out to God, open God's
Word at the same time. Take a psalm and pray through it.
Colossians 3:16 tells us that God's Word is to dwell in us
richly. Surely one of the most rewarding ways to fulfill that
command is in prayer.

He Prayed Despite Overwhelming Obstacles

Jonah's prayer had to overcome several barriers. First,
he knew it was God, not really the sailors, who threw him

into the ocean. He said, "For Thou hadst cast me into the deep. . . . All Thy breakers and billows passed over me" (Jon. 2:3).

Because Jonah knew the Lord was responsible for casting him into the sea, I think he was tempted not to pray. At this point in the prophet's life, God was his adversary, not his advocate, so how could he ask him for help?

The fourth verse explains Jonah's dilemma further: "So I said, 'I have been expelled from Thy sight. Nevertheless I will look again toward Thy holy temple.'"

What perseverance! If you were convinced that God had expelled you from his sight, would you have the courage to pray? What good would it do? Jonah thought the Lord was finished with him, yet he said, "Nevertheless I will look again toward Thy holy temple." He overcame his obstacle.

As if this weren't enough, Jonah encountered other barriers that could have discouraged him from praying. Look at verses 5 and 6:

> "Water encompassed me to the point of death.
> The great deep engulfed me.
> Weeds were wrapped around my head.
> I descended to the roots of the mountains.
> The earth with its bars was around me forever."

That's what I call a hopeless situation. Jonah testified that seaweed was wrapped around his head and water was engulfing him. Although he spent three days and nights inside the fish, the prophet described it as being forever. He saw no end to his problem. He thought he was doomed for sure.

But still he prayed. He did not allow his many obstacles to break down his communication with God.

What is hindering your crying out to the Lord? Are you under circumstances that look impossible to conquer? Then all the more opportunity for Christ to receive glory when he acts. If Jonah could pray despite his problem, can't you and I? The prophet thought God was his enemy, but we know Christ is our friend. He proved that when he died on the cross. And yet we allow molehill problems to become mountains of discouragement to our prayers.

He Prayed with Confession of Sin

In verse 8 Jonah made this confession to God: "Those who regard vain idols forsake their faithfulness."

The Living Bible makes this difficult verse simple to understand. It says, "Those who worship false gods have turned their backs on all the mercies waiting for them from the Lord!" That's exactly what Jonah had done. When the ship was in danger, he refused to call on the Lord for help. The mariners had cried out to their heathen gods, but it was an exercise in futility. And because Jonah in effect depended on their prayers to vain idols, he deprived himself of all the mercies God had in store for him. Instead of deliverance, he found disaster.

But once in the belly of the fish, Jonah confessed his sin. Sometimes in our prayers we conceal our sins. We tell the Lord, "I know I lost my temper this morning, but it was all the fault of my children. They got on my nerves." Or we say, "Yes, Father, I know I told a lie today, but I also witnessed to three people. Aren't you happy about that?" However, complaining or glossing over our sins is not the same as confessing them.

For twenty–two years a Christian couple I know had problems in their marriage. They sought counseling from a psychologist, who told them after several sessions that the husband simply was not a "one-woman man." A divorce soon followed. Instead of confessing his sin, this man excused himself on the basis that he wasn't cut out to be a faithful husband, as if God had made him that way. I wonder how far that excuse will get him on judgment day.

Maybe your pit of trouble is sin. Like Jonah in the fish's stomach, you are in the grip of Satan. You want to live in a way that pleases God, but you can't, because your sinful nature is dominating you. You may be convinced that you will never be able to change. Then remember Jonah. His outlook was hopeless, too. But when he confessed his sin, God delivered him. And the Lord is willing to rescue you, also, from the greatest of all problems—sin. That was Jesus' purpose in coming to earth and dying on Calvary's cross.

He Prayed Thankfully

In the ninth verse Jonah prayed,

> "But I will sacrifice to Thee
> With the voice of thanksgiving.
> That which I have vowed I will pay.
> Salvation is from the LORD."

The prophet, remember, was still in the great fish when he said those words. He was filled with thanks even though he had not yet been delivered, because he still had something to be thankful about. He praised God for salvation. That mattered more to Jonah than physical deliverance from the pit of the sea monster.

When he said, "Salvation is from the LORD," I think he meant, "If it weren't for you, Lord, I would still be spiritually out of touch. If you had allowed my ship to travel safely to Tarshish, I might never have prayed again. Thank you for saving me from that. Thank you for the storm."

If this runaway missionary could praise God for his trial, we can do the same. Sometimes we are poor at spiritual arithmetic—we can hardly count our blessings. But if we look for our Lord's hand in all our ordeals, we will discover abundant cause for thanksgiving.

When I was age seventeen my doctor informed me that I was diabetic. I was rushed to the hospital, where they told me I would have to give myself injections every day for the rest of my life. My eating habits would have to change. If not careful I could die. Hearing these things I was devastated.

A friend of mine from church visited me in the hospital. She made a get-well card and handed it to me. After she left that night, I opened it. On the outside of the card were the words of 1 Thessalonians 5:16–18, "Rejoice always; pray without ceasing; in everything give thanks; for this is God's will for you in Christ Jesus."

When I turned to the inside of the card, I found these words: "Tom, have you thanked the Lord yet?"

I was convicted. I immediately bowed my head and said, "Thank you, Father, that my diabetes does not change anything between you and me. I know you still love me, and I still love you, too. Help me to learn and grow through this daily discipline. I place my life in your hands. Use me for your glory. Amen."

That was one of the most fulfilling prayers of my life. In over two decades since then I've been reminded every day as I take my insulin injections and eat my meals that I'm dependent on the Lord for health. Diabetes has caused me to understand my mortality and has prevented me from taking life or my Lord for granted. Though it does have its trials, it is something I can be thankful for.

The opposite of a thankful heart is a bitter one. Bitterness will devour you from the inside out. Thankfulness will season your life and turn your trials into triumphs.

He Prayed with a Repentant Heart

Jonah did not ask the Lord for one thing in this prayer. He didn't even mention the fish. Instead, he admitted he deserved all the discipline God had dished out.

How can we know if we are truly repentant? If we are only sorry we got caught in sin, that's not enough. A person's desire to escape God's punishment does not make him repentant. Criminals would love to avoid going to prison, but does that mean they are sorry for their crimes? Repentance is seen when we grieve over hurting God personally, when we are more sorry for his sake than for ours.

That's how Jonah felt. He was not angry at himself for failing to outwit God. He was ashamed of himself for letting his Lord down. His biggest problem was not that he was in the stomach of the fish but that as Jehovah's prophet he had given a poor testimony to the sailors. He had failed his Lord.

Sometimes when we are down in the pit of trouble we ask, "How could God allow this to happen to me?" We can even resent the Lord for our problems. If you've been in the stomach of a great fish lately, ask yourself, "Am I to blame for my predicament?" That's a question we easily overlook. Not all our problems come as discipline for our disobedience, but some do. If it could happen to Jonah, it can happen to us.

He Prayed Successfully

Finally, Jonah's prayer was one that the Lord granted. Almost immediately Jonah was aware of an answer: "I called out of my distress to the LORD, and He answered me" (Jon. 2:2).

The most obvious answer to his prayer is found in the tenth verse: "Then the LORD commanded the fish, and it vomited Jonah up onto the dry land."

From a worldly point of view, we might say the fish couldn't stomach Jonah! I heard of a Sunday school teacher who asked her class, "What do we learn from the story of Jonah and the fish?"

A little girl quickly raised her hand and replied, "We learn that people make whales sick."

Fortunately, there is something more to learn than that. We also discover that God wants to give specific answers to our prayers. I can just see Jonah as he brushed the sand off his body after landing on the beach. He would look back at the gigantic fish, only to notice it flick its tail at him, as if it were saying, "Good riddance!" And then he would think to himself, "God is speaking to me even in that." He would learn that following the Lord is easier than running away from him, that his disobedience did not pay, that God's love for him was tough, and that Jehovah specializes in the impossible.

How seriously do we expect answers to our prayers? When we send a letter to a friend asking for a favor, we look for a reply in the mail. But when God says yes to our prayers, we are surprised.

I remember telling a friend about an answer to one of my prayers. Then I remarked, "It's a miracle!"

He only replied, "Isn't that the business God is in?"

Yes, it is. So let's voice specific prayers, fulfill clear conditions, exercise childlike faith, and then wait for God to send a specific answer. Surely that attitude pleases him, because it shows commitment to the Lord and trust in his goodness.

Personal Application

You cannot see the stars in the daytime unless you go down into a well. Jonah's example teaches us that God sometimes drops us into wells of trouble in order to draw us close to himself. If it weren't for that deep pit, we would never have looked up and seen the Lord. Instead, we would have been satisfied to be worldly minded and blind to his majesty.

Jonah's story is every believer's story. At this point in your life you may be trapped in the belly of your own sea monster. It may be a marriage that has gone sour, or maybe one that was bad from the beginning because you defied God in your choice of a mate. But now you're stuck.

The Lord delivered Jonah from his fish, although even that was a traumatic experience. Verse 10 says it "vomited" him up onto the dry land.

Often, however, God does not deliver us out of our problem. Instead, he wants to lift the problem out of us. Either way, he desires to show himself trustworthy even in the midst of our troubles. Many heroes in Scripture learned this lesson. Joseph had it brought home to him when his brothers sold him into Egyptian slavery. Jeremiah realized it when he was abandoned in a muddy cistern. Shadrach, Meshach, and Abednego discovered this truth about God when they were pushed into Nebuchadnezzar's fiery furnace. Daniel learned it when God required him to spend a night in the lions' den. And the apostle Paul came to this conclusion when the heavenly Father refused to heal him of a thorn in his flesh.

Whether God takes you out of the problem or the problem out of you, remember that you can cry to him for help. The secret to gaining his help is to be willing to let the heavenly Father deal with you *his* way. That's the primary lesson from the prayer life of Jonah.

13

The Prayer Life of Christ

*His Life Was a Prayer,
and Prayer Was His Life*

No doubt the foremost prayer warrior in all the Bible is Jesus Christ. The four Gospels record seventeen specific examples of his prayers. Curiously, it takes less than ten minutes to read them all. And yet Scripture says he also invested entire nights in prayer.

The Gospel of John presents us with some good examples of Jesus in prayer, including his longest recorded one. But it never uses the words *prayer* or *pray*. The nearest equivalent is *ask*. Perhaps John wanted us to see that Christ's life was a prayer, and prayer was his life.

Rather than examine Jesus' seventeen prayers one at a

153

time, we will look at the composite picture and cull general principles from his habits of prayer.

For Jesus Prayer Was Important

To many Christians prayer is a spiritual life preserver. In the case of an emergency it's the first thing we reach for. But in our daily circumstances we store that life preserver away.

"But He Himself would often slip away to the wilderness and pray" (Luke 5:16). Underscore that word *often*. Far from wearing prayer like a life preserver, our Lord dressed himself in it every day. Mark 1:35 tells us that "in the early morning, while it was still dark, He arose and went out and departed to a lonely place, and was praying there."

Many people have told me they would like to have consistent times of conversation with God, but they are just too busy. Jesus was also busy. If he were going to spend quality time with the Father in his mornings, he had to get up before dawn, and he did.

I recommend meeting with God the first part of your day. Waiting until bedtime to pray is like practicing for the baseball game after the ninth inning or studying the textbook after the exam. If you want to show the Lord that he is special to you, put him first in your day, just as Jesus did. In Luke 6:12 we find these words: "And it was at this time that He went off to the mountain to pray, and He spent the whole night in prayer to God."

Have you ever spent an entire night in prayer? I know others who have, but I have not done so. I have spent whole nights catching up on my sleep, worrying, and dreaming about some goal I wanted to accomplish. Those three things represent important matters in my life. Jesus prayed all night because it was important to him. His private life was the secret of his public life.

For Jesus Prayer Was Influential

Our Savior's prayers exercised a powerful influence on different groups of persons. First, they influenced his disciples. "And it came about that while He was praying in a certain place, after He had finished, one of His disciples said to Him, 'Lord, teach us to pray'" (Luke 11:1).

As far as we know from Scripture, the disciples never asked Jesus to teach them to preach, heal, or perform miracles. But at least one of them said, "Teach us to pray." There was something attractive about Jesus' prayer life. People who loved him wanted to share this quality. Even today we believers read the prayers of Christ with a holy fascination. They influence us, too.

Yet we often despair of having a prayer life anything like our Lord's. Consequently, we make puny requests of him. If our hearts would speak, they would say to Christ, "Teach us to make money" or "Teach us to be successful." We might get a little more spiritual and request lessons on controlling our tempers, living cheerfully with pain, or becoming a more loving husband, a more submissive wife, or a more understanding parent. But our real need is to know God more intimately, so we must dare to say, "Teach me to pray."

Jesus' prayers not only influenced his disciples, they influenced the other members of the Trinity.

> Now it came about when all the people were baptized, that Jesus also was baptized, and while He was praying, heaven was opened, and the Holy Spirit descended upon Him in bodily form like a dove, and a voice came out of heaven,

"Thou art My beloved Son, in Thee I am well-pleased"
(Luke 3:21, 22).

Here Christ's prayer opened heaven, brought the Spirit
on him, and caused the heavenly Father to speak. George
Müller left a lifelong record of his prayers and their
answers—about 25,000 of them. When a friend asked him
to explain his secret, he replied, "Have faith in God."

Do you believe all heaven responds to your prayers? If
not, that could explain why you have received no answers.
"Without faith it is impossible to please Him" (Heb. 11:6).

Third, Jesus' prayers influenced himself. "And while He
was praying, the appearance of His face became different,
and His clothing became white and gleaming" (Luke 9:29).

We call this the transfiguration of Christ. His example
teaches us that prayer transforms our characters. Of
course Jesus was already perfect. His transfiguration was
only an unveiling of the heavenly glory he already possessed. But for us glorification is a process. God wants us
to grow in holiness, and prayer is one of the means he has
established to help us do that.

Often the question is asked, "Does prayer change
things?" Yes, it does. But even more than things, prayer
changes us. Once you enter God's presence, you cannot
leave as the same person. Like Christ's in his transfiguration, Moses' face glowed after he met with God in the
Tabernacle (Exod. 34:34, 35). And Jesus commands us to
let our lights shine before people, that they might give
glory to God (Matt. 5:16). If we are going to shine, then as
did Jesus and Moses we must speak to God in prayer.

Fourth, the Bible reveals that Jesus' prayers influenced
nonbelievers. When he stood in front of the tomb of his
friend, Lazarus, "Jesus raised His eyes, and said, 'Father, I

thank Thee that Thou heardest Me. And I knew that Thou hearest Me always; but because of the people standing around I said it, that they may believe that Thou didst send Me'" (John 11:41, 42).

Note the purpose of that prayer—that people might believe. Our Lord's next words were, "Lazarus, come forth." And out he came, graveclothes and all! The result is found in verse 45: "Many therefore of the Jews, who had come to Mary and beheld what He had done, believed in Him." Two miracles occurred that day. Not only did a dead man walk out of his tomb, but people dead in sin received spiritual life. Jesus' prayer request was granted.

How do you change friends and family members who refuse to trust in Christ? You don't. Only God can accomplish that. But as a means toward that end you can pray for them. That's what God honors for the conversion of non-Christians.

Finally, notice that Jesus' prayers influenced Satan. In Luke 22:31, 32 our Lord told Peter, "Simon, Simon, behold, Satan has demanded permission to sift you like wheat; but I have prayed for you, that your faith may not fail."

We may think, "There's one petition that wasn't granted, because Peter did fail miserably that same night." True, Peter failed, but his faith did not, and that's what Jesus prayed for. Even though Peter denied knowing Christ, his faith caused him to repent and seek reconciliation with the Master (John 21:15–17). Surely the two New Testament letters Peter wrote also prove that his faith did not fail.

Satan's aim was not merely to disgrace Peter, but also to destroy him. Satan requested permission to sift the apostle like wheat. Commentator William Hendriksen explains that in the ancient sifting process, a person, usually a woman:

grasps a sieve in both hands, and begins to shake it vigorously from side to side so that the chaff will rise to the surface. This is then thrown away. Next, she puts that sieve through a teeter-totter motion, raising now this and then that side, and blowing over it, so that what still remains of the chaff gathers in an easily removable pile (William Hendriksen, *The Gospel of Luke* [Grand Rapids: Baker Book House, 1978], p. 973).

The devil received his permission to sift Peter, and the apostle was tested that same night with satanic violence. But even before the enemy began his assault, Jesus prayed. And because he prayed, Satan was unable to achieve his goal of destroying Peter. Thus, prayer influences even the devil.

For Jesus Prayer Was Intense

The night of our Lord's arrest, he led his disciples out to the Mount of Olives, one of his favorite places of prayer.

And He knelt down and began to pray, saying, "Father, if Thou art willing, remove this cup from Me; yet not My will, but Thine be done." Now an angel from heaven appeared to Him, strengthening Him. And being in agony He was praying very fervently; and His sweat became like drops of blood, falling down upon the ground (Luke 22:41–44).

Here is omnipotent God needing an angel to strengthen him. The text also says he was in agony. Only one thing could cause that. Our Lord was thinking ahead to the next day, when he would be crucified and bear the punishment for the sins of the world. No wonder Jesus sweat great drops of blood. Here we see the willingness of Christ to become the sacrifice for our sins. The nails had not yet pierced his hands and feet. The spear had not yet been thrust into his side. But he already was shedding his blood. What love!

There is nothing like the thought of death to intensify our prayers. People who have survived airline crashes testify that when they thought they were going to die, they prayed as never before. Jesus, however, was facing much more than death. After all, many people have died bravely. What brought our Lord into agony of spirit, weakness, and sweating of blood was the thought of enduring all the pains of hell. This was the greatest trial of his life, and Luke says he met it by "praying very fervently."

How do you respond to a crisis? Some people worry. Others accuse God of cruelty and nurse a bitter spirit against him. Jesus teaches us by example that the proper response to a crisis is prayer—not just rattling off a grocery list of demands or requests but an intense yielding of yourself to the heavenly Father's will.

Another example of Jesus' intensity in prayer is found in Matthew 27:46. He had been hanging on the cross for six hours. It was three o'clock in the afternoon. Since noon the sky had been black, because the heavenly Father had turned his back on his Son, who had been made into our sin. Just then "Jesus cried out with a loud voice, saying, 'ELI, ELI, LAMA SABACHTHANI?' that is, 'MY GOD, MY GOD, WHY HAST THOU FORSAKEN ME?'"

Many a widow and widower knows the awful loneliness that sets in after a spouse dies. Some have lived together for fifty, sixty, or more years, and those who are left feel as if they've been cut in half. But even they can glean only an inkling of Jesus' pain, for he was severed from the heavenly Father. No one has ever enjoyed the

love of God more than Christ. Nor has anyone ever loved
the Father in return as much as he. But here for the first
time in all eternity, Jesus was cut off from him. When the
light of God's face turned to darkness, it was surely the
most painful and depressing experience that even Christ
could feel. For the time being at least, even he does not
understand it. All he can do is cry out, "Why?"

Maybe you have lost a child in a tragic death that made
no sense. Perhaps someone you love was paralyzed in an
accident or is suffering from cancer or AIDS. The one
question that nags at your heart is, "Why?" Take comfort
in this: Even Jesus asked God, "Why?" He did it intensely,
in a loud voice.

There are two ways to ask that question. One is to call
God to account and demand an answer. The other is to
cast yourself on him as your comforter. I think it signifi-
cant that Christ did not ask, "God, God, why hast Thou
forsaken Me?" Instead, he said, "My God, My God, why?"
Even in his hour of greatest pain, he was still claiming the
Father as his own! I'm sure Satan was tempting him to let
go, but through the intensity of prayer he continued to
hang on.

Do you know why we don't hang on? Because we have
not learned how to pray intensely. Prayer is like a fire—it
is meant to burn. The droopy-eyed, lukewarm mumblings
we call prayer invite God to deny our requests.

William Law once said, "It is not the arithmetic of our
prayers, how many they are; nor the rhetoric of our
prayers, how eloquent they are; nor the geometry of our
prayers, how long they are; nor the logic of our prayers,
how argumentative they are; nor the method of our
prayers, how orderly they are, that God cares about.
Fervency of spirit is what captures His heart."

For Jesus Prayer Was Intercessory

We have already seen several examples of Jesus' inter-cession for others, such as his prayer at the tomb of Lazarus that people might believe, and his plea that Peter's faith would not fail the test of Satan's sieve. But there is more.

The entire seventeenth chapter of John records a prayer of Christ filled with intercession. In it he asked the following:

> That they may know Thee, the only true God, and Jesus Christ whom Thou hast sent (v. 3); I ask on their behalf (v. 9); keep them in Thy name (v. 11); keep them from the evil one (v. 15); Sanctify them in the truth (v. 17); I do not ask in behalf of these alone, but for those also who believe in Me through their word; that they may all be one (vv. 20, 21); that the world may believe that Thou didst send Me (v. 21); that they may be one, just as We are one (v. 22); that they may be perfected in unity (v. 23); I desire that they also, whom Thou hast given Me, be with Me where I am, in order that they may behold My glory (v. 24).

In that twentieth verse Jesus prayed for everyone who would eventually believe through the apostles' witness, found in the pages of the New Testament. Just think, nearly 20 centuries ago you were on Christ's prayer list! And you will remain on it until he comes again, because even now in heaven "He always lives to make intercession for them" (Heb. 7:25).

Perhaps the most exceptional example of our Lord's intercession is found in Luke 23:34. After his enemies nailed him to the cross, "Jesus was saying, 'Father, forgive them; for they do not know what they are doing.'"

Even in his moment of greatest pain and suffering, our

Lord was not only thinking of others but praying for them. And these were his murderers, not his friends! The last martyr in Old Testament history was Zechariah, the son of a priest named Jehoiada. "Zechariah's last words as he died were 'Lord, see what they are doing and pay them back'" (2 Chron. 24:22 LB). That's how most of us would respond if we were being murdered. We would ask God to punish the guilty. Jesus, however, begged for their pardon.

This is why it is meaningful to pray "in Jesus' name." When we do that, we are telling the heavenly Father, "My pleas for the lost are an echo of Jesus' intercession for them. Because he asked you to pardon unbelievers, I am confident you will grant my prayers for them, too."

The prayer of Christ from the cross was repeated in the death of the first Christian martyr, Stephen. While rocks from an angry mob crushed against his skull, he said with his dying breath, "Lord, do not hold this sin against them!" (Acts 7:60). That is proof that he was filled with the Spirit of Christ.

This is what God is looking for in you and me—a heart that is emptied of self and filled with compassion for others; a heart that aches to see people know Jesus and receive his forgiveness; a heart that will die if only others might find life in the Savior.

By the way, was Christ's prayer answered? Yes, God did forgive Jesus' executioners. Mark 15:39 reports that "when the centurion, who was standing right in front of Him, saw the way He breathed His last, he said, 'Truly this man was the Son of God!'" That is a humble profession of faith. And about seven weeks later, three thousand Jews—some, no doubt, who had been responsible for Christ's death—heard the message of salvation and repented of their sins (Acts 2:41).

And what about Stephen's prayer? Were his murderers forgiven, as he requested? We know of one prominent one who was—Saul, who later became the apostle Paul. Hundreds of years ago Augustine put it this way: "If Stephen had not prayed, the church would not have had the apostle Paul."

Personal Application

Surely God would not want us to examine Jesus' prayer life in a theoretical or merely academic sense. First Peter 2:21 teaches that Christ left an example for us, that we might follow in his steps. We can be sure the prayer life of Christ should become the basis for our prayer life. We are not meant to admire it so much as to apply it.

For Jesus, prayer was important, influential, intense, and intercessory. Maybe those adjectives do not describe your prayer life right now. But don't despair. The making of a prayer warrior does not take place overnight. Are you willing to take the first step? Will you settle it in your heart and life that from this point on prayer will be important to you?

You may have to readjust your thinking or even your theology about prayer. You will have to schedule specific periods in the day for quiet times with God. And you may well need to keep a prayer list of specific requests and answers from God.

If you begin at step one and make prayer an important part of your spiritual life, steps two through four in the prayer life of Christ will naturally follow. The heavenly Father will cause your petitions to influence all kinds of people, even Satan himself. You will become dissatisfied with cold, indifferent requests. Your prayers will glow with intensity! And selfishness will more and more be overcome, resulting in a ministry of intercession for others. In short, your life will become a prayer, and prayer will become your life.

Does that seem to be an unrealistic goal? Not for someone who is filled with the Spirit of the living Christ.

14

The Prayer Life of Paul
Focusing on Spiritual Needs

How spiritual are your prayers? Often our conversations with God focus on physical and material needs rather than spiritual ones. The average Christian's prayer might run something like this:

> Dear God, please relieve my arthritis pain this morning. And give my husband safety as he travels today. Don't let my son get hurt in the football game this afternoon (and please let his team win). And Lord, help us to find the money to pay our bills.

Now don't get me wrong. Not one of these petitions is out of line. God invites us to make our requests known to him in prayer (Phil. 4:6). He wants us to unburden our hearts. But the prayer could stand improvement. It's top-heavy with physical, material, and worldly matters. It needs to be balanced with spiritual concerns. Here is an example of how that might be done:

> Dear God, by Your all-sufficient grace help me to be cheerful with people in spite of my arthritis pain. Fill my husband with your Spirit so that he can represent Christ in his work today. Thank you that my son can enjoy football, but don't let it become a substitute for you in his worship. And continue to teach my husband and me to practice faithful stewardship and then trust you to meet our financial needs.

If ever a man knew how to plead with God for the spiritual needs of others, it was the apostle Paul. This is not to say he didn't pray about physical needs. Three times he asked the Lord to remove his thorn in the flesh (2 Cor. 12:8). He once spent all night and the next day treading water in the sea (2 Cor. 11:25), and I'm sure he prayed during that experience for someone to rescue him. But for the most part Paul's prayer life focused on spiritual needs. His New Testament letters are chock-full of examples. We shall look at nine of them.

The Need for Spiritual Life

In Romans 10:1 Paul wrote, concerning the unbelieving Jews of his day,

"Brethren, my heart's desire and my prayer to God for them is for their salvation." Are you praying regularly for the salvation of someone you know who is apart from Christ? This is every person's first and most important spiritual need.

The Jews had chased Paul out of one city after another, slandered him in courts of law, thrown him into prisons, plotted to ambush him in cold blood, and even stoned him. How would you feel toward them if you were Paul? Unforgiving? Bitter? Paul yearned for their salvation. How could he do that? Because he understood that their hatred of him was caused by their alienation from Christ. He knew that in the final analysis the Jews were not fighting against him but against his Lord. They had a spiritual problem with Christ, not a clash of personalities with Paul. Therefore, he fought *for* them in prayer, not *against* them as enemies. His only enemy was the devil.

A woman I'll call Jennifer learned that her husband was committing adultery. Naturally, she felt deeply hurt. For a while she sulked as the victim of her husband's offense. Then I asked her, "Who died for Jim's sin?"

"Jesus, of course," was her reply.

"Then *he* is the real victim, not *you*." When I said that, her eyes lit up. For the first time she was able to place herself outside the problem. And from that point on, her prayers changed from "Lord, help *me* to get over my pain," to "Lord, help *Jim* to quit fighting against you." Instead of praying for her own emotional need, she began interceding compassionately for her husband's spiritual need. The result? Her bitterness toward her husband soon melted, and she began loving him again.

The Need for Spiritual Vision

In Ephesians 1:18 Paul writes, "I pray that the eyes of your heart may be enlightened." Notice that our hearts have eyes. Once, when Christ was traveling down a road, the crowd spoke of him as "Jesus of Nazareth." To them he was just a man. But a blind man in that crowd, Bartimaeus, called him Jesus, Son of David (Luke 18:37, 38). He alone saw Christ as the Messiah.

In the ninth chapter of John, the Pharisees confidently

said of Jesus, "We know that this man is a sinner" (John 9:24). But a man who had been born blind "said, 'Lord, I believe.' And he worshiped Him" (John 9:38).

Ironically, people with no eyesight often had the most insight into Jesus Christ. That's because God has given people the ability to see with their hearts. (Sadly, the only vision some Christians practice is television.) In Psalm 119:18 David prayed, "Open my eyes, that I may behold wonderful things from Thy law." That's the kind of sight we so desperately need.

Paul says this spiritual vision will enable us to "know what is the hope of His calling, what are the riches of the glory of His inheritance in the saints, and what is the surpassing greatness of His power toward us who believe" (Eph. 1:18, 19).

Clearly, all those things represent spiritual needs. That's what mattered most to Paul.

The Need for Spiritual Power

Ephesians 3 provides us with another example from Paul's prayer life. He writes: "I bow my knees before the Father . . . that He would grant you, according to the riches of His glory, to be strengthened with power through His Spirit in the inner man" (Eph. 3:14, 16).

We tend to overlook our inner persons. We emphasize our outward selves. Satan does not care if we are well fed, well clothed, popular, rich, and beautiful, if only he can have our hearts, our inner persons.

In the Bible, Samson was strong on the outside, but weak on the inside. He could kill three thousand Philistines in one afternoon, but he was powerless against his inward lusts. All his physical needs were met, but spiritually he was as weak as water.

In contrast to Samson, Daniel as a mere youth resolved not to defile himself with a pagan king's food and customs. He did not look powerful—he was only a teenager —but his inward strength made him one of the mightiest heroes in the Bible.

So how do we become spiritually strong? By mustering up our willpower? No! We've tried that a thousand times, and it has never worked. Paul's prayer says the inner man is strengthened "through His [God's] Spirit." That means we must yield ourselves to the Holy Spirit's control.

Most Christians have a survival mentality when it comes to strengthening the inner person. As long as we have the assurance that our sins are forgiven and we're on our way to heaven, we are willing to forfeit everyday spiritual battles. It doesn't matter to us that our lives are carnal, unfruitful, and dishonoring to God. Someone has said that if the heavenly Father withdrew his Spirit from this world, most Christians would go right on doing what they've always been doing—and no one would know the difference. That's the survival mentality. And people who possess it are in spiritual need. They require strengthening of the inner person.

The Need for Spiritual Fellowship

Paul's next request for his readers is "that Christ may dwell in your hearts through faith" (Eph. 3:17).

We may wonder if Christians already have Christ dwelling in their hearts. Yes, they do. The Greek word for *dwell* in this verse means "home" in its noun form. The Living Bible paraphrases it this way: "I pray that Christ will be more and more at home in your hearts." Paul asks that "Christ might finally settle down and feel completely at home in your hearts."

Not everyone who knocks on your front door gets all the way into your home. You may talk to a deliveryman out on the doorstep, because he's a stranger. Others you invite into the living room, but no farther. However, when your children come in, they have the run of the whole house.

How far does Jesus Christ get into the home of your heart? How much spiritual fellowship do you enjoy with him? Have you left him waiting out on the front doorstep? Maybe you've invited him in, but he's still sitting as a visitor in the living room. Or have you turned the key, the deed, and full authority over to him?

I'm reminded of Robert Munger's booklet, *My Heart, Christ's Home.* In vivid storytelling fashion he pictures each area of his life as a room in his heart in which Jesus lives. The library is his thought life and reading material. The living room stands for his pleasures. The kitchen represents his appetites, the family room his relationships, the closet his secret life, and so forth. At first Jesus comes into the home of his heart as a guest. Then gradually he is given the keys to each room. One by one the author hands over the separate areas of his life to the Lord. The story pictures exactly what Paul is praying for in this verse—that Christ might settle down and feel completely comfortable in the home of our hearts. That was the spiritual need of the Ephesians, and today it is our need.

The Need for Spiritual Depth

Next, the apostle asks that his readers might be "rooted and grounded in love" (Eph. 3:17).

Here are two metaphors, one from agriculture (rooted), and the other from architecture (grounded). Each emphasizes depth, since you cannot see the roots of a tree or the foundation of a building; they are hidden underground. But without them there is no stability.

Love is the common denominator in both illustrations. It's the soil into which we must sink our roots and the foundation on which we must build our lives.

How deep is your spiritual life? Far too many Christians are shallow. And too many churches have a superficial love for and commitment to the Lord. It's when the trials come our way that we discover our spiritual depth and firmness. Storms cannot topple trees with deep roots or buildings with firm foundations. Nor can the storms of tragedy, disease, and grief cause the faith of a mature Christian to collapse. His roots sink too deeply into the soil of Christ's love. He's founded on the bedrock of that love. And that gives him stability.

The Need for Spiritual Comprehension

Paul goes on to ask God, in Ephesians 3:18, 19, that we "may be able to comprehend with all the saints what is the breadth and length and height and depth, and to know the love of Christ which surpasses knowledge."

The word *comprehend* means "to make one's own." It speaks of experiencing something firsthand—in this case, the love of Christ. Every child of God knows that Jesus loves him. We read it in the Bible, hear pastors preach on it, and listen to others bear witness to it. But that's like reading or hearing about the nourishment of a good meal. It makes sense, but it falls far short of actually sitting down to the table and eating the meal. Our faith in Christ is meant to be not theory but practice. Our Lord wants us to understand his great love with our hearts, not just our heads.

To many people Christ's love is a sentimental belief on

the level of a fairy tale. To others it's pure conjecture. And to some it's a joke. But for Paul it was a substantial fact. He spoke of it as something you can measure. It has a "breadth and length and height and depth."

John 3:16 illustrates those dimensions: "For God so loved the world [the breadth of God's love], that He gave His only begotten Son [the length to which his love went], that whoever believes in Him should not perish [the depth of God's love], but have eternal life [the glorious height of God's love]."

Paradoxically, after making his request that we understand the love of Christ, Paul adds that it "surpasses knowledge." (G. K. Chesterton once defined a paradox as "truth standing on its head to attract attention.")

Precisely because we can never know the love of Christ fully in this life, we must set out to fathom its depth, scale its height, walk its length, and measure its breadth. That was Paul's prayer request for the Ephesians. Is it your heart's desire and prayer to God—both for yourself and for others you love?

The Need for Spiritual Fulness

Again, the apostle asks the Lord that his fellow believers "may be filled up to all the fulness of God" (Eph. 3:19).

What a request! To fill a human being with God's fulness is like trying to cram the Pacific Ocean into a child's cup. But look at it in this light: We are the body of Christ. And "in Him all the fulness of Deity dwells in bodily form" (Col. 2:9). The only Christ many people will ever see is the one in us. And God wants them to see all of him! He yearns for the world to get a full picture of the living Lord Jesus in the lives of us, his people. So we must fill ourselves with the Word of Christ, the Spirit of Christ, and the love of Christ.

Beware of spiritual emptiness. Avoid wasted days (especially Sundays), spiritually hollow friends, the mind that is barren of Scripture, and the heart that is blank in prayer. Nature abhors a vacuum. If our lives are void of spiritual good, evil will rush in, and we won't be empty for long.

God knows we're going to be filled with something, so he tells us to fill up on him. And not just for our own sakes, but that we might overflow with Christ's love. Our Lord doesn't fill us so we can have spiritual indigestion. He pours himself out into our hearts so that we might spill over into the hearts of empty, hurting, and needy people.

The Need for Spiritual Maturity

In another of Paul's prayers he writes, "This we also pray for, that you be made complete" (2 Cor. 13:9).

The word *complete* means "mature." The Living Bible paraphrases it this way: "Our greatest wish and prayer is that you will become mature Christians."

Not long ago a woman asked me, "How can I know if I'm growing spiritually?"

"By the evidence of spiritual fruit in your life," I replied. I then reminded her of Galatians 5:22, 23: "But the fruit of the Spirit is love, joy, peace, patience, kindness, goodness, faithfulness, gentleness, self-control." We could add other traits: a consistent and unselfish prayer life, spiritual wisdom that results from a daily intake of the Word of God, a walk of faith, regular fellowship with other believers, a stewardship mentality, an acceptance of trials as divine tools to shape us into the image of Christ, and practical service to our Lord. These are the marks of maturity. Unlike Jonah's plant, they don't grow quickly. But they do continue to grow throughout our lives.

Warren Wiersbe writes: "Spiritual maturity is one of the greatest needs in churches today. Too many churches are playpens for babies instead of workshops for adults. After over a quarter century of ministry, I am convinced that spiritual immaturity is the number one problem in our churches. God is looking for mature men and women to carry on His work, and sometimes all He can find are little children who cannot even get along with each other" (*Bible Exposition Commentary*, 2:336).

I heard about a high school principal who promoted one of his teachers with ten years of experience to an administrative post. When the announcement was made, another teacher protested, "Why did you give him this position? He has only ten years of experience, and I have twenty-five years!"

The principal wagged his head and said, "I'm sorry, but you're wrong. You don't have twenty-five years of experience. You've had one year's experience repeated twenty-five times."

Some people have been Christians for twenty-five years, but they have matured only a year's worth, or less. As a result, the Lord may send them trials to teach them the same lessons over and over again. They have never grown in their Christian lives. Are you like that? If so, you have a spiritual need worth praying about.

The Need for Spiritual Love

In Philippians 1:9 we read another of Paul's requests: "And this I pray, that your love may abound."

Nothing is more satisfying in life than loving someone. Every bride and groom knows this on their wedding day.

Most parents understand it as they watch their children grow up. But sadly, many people have neglected to love Christ. The first complaint in Christ's letters to the seven churches of Asia is, "You have left your first love" (Rev. 2:4).

Do you love Jesus enough to die for him? Do you cultivate your love for Christ by daily Bible study and prayer, speaking of him with other people, and regular, consistent worship? If you cannot answer yes to these questions, you have a spiritual need that calls for earnest prayer.

Personal Application

Our survey of these nine sample prayers from Paul's life reveals the lack of spiritual requests in my own prayer life, and I suspect in yours, too.

So let me recommend a two-week experiment. Every morning of the first week take Paul's prayer in Ephesians 1:18, 19 and pray it for yourself. And every evening that week do the same with Ephesians 3:16–19. Whenever Paul writes *you*, substitute *I* or *me*. And change his word *your* to *my*.

In the second week let these prayers be your requests for someone else—maybe a family member or a close friend. Intercede for that person using Paul's words from Ephesians 1:18, 19 in the morning and Ephesians 3:16–19 in the evening. Then see if this two-week experiment doesn't transform your prayer practice in the future. I believe it will.

Some time ago I received a letter from Paul Gross, a friend of mine. It was so unusual that I saved it.

Dear Tom,

The Lord brought you to mind this morning, so I prayed for you. I asked God to count you worthy of his calling. I also prayed that by his power he may fulfill your every

good purpose and every act which is prompted by your faith. I prayed this so that the name of Jesus may be glorified in you and you in him, according to the grace of our heavenly Father and the Lord Jesus Christ.
I love you in the Lord,

Paul

As you can imagine, receiving that letter made my day. What put that prayer in a class by itself was that each one of its requests focused on spiritual needs. Paul Gross is a man who has captured the heart of Paul the apostle. I believe God wants you and me to do the same.

15

Your Prayer Life

Practicing the Principles of the Lord's Prayer

The best-known prayer ever uttered is the Lord's Prayer. You can find it in Matthew 6:9–13. Some Bible teachers have said it's wrong to call this our Lord's prayer, because Jesus would never have said, "Forgive us our debts." But because our Lord gave us this prayer, we can call it his, in the same sense that I might say, "Did you receive *my* letter in the mail?"

Many Christians recite this prayer in tape-recorder fashion. They press a button, and out come the words. No thought. No understanding. No heart in it. Just words mumbled into the air that quickly fall to the ground.

In his preface to this prayer, Jesus said, "Pray, then, in this way" (Matt. 6:9).

That means we are to take this prayer as more of a model than a script to be memorized. Our Lord wants us to glean principles from it and build our prayer lives on them. Look with me at ten of these principles.

Pray through Jesus Christ

The prayer begins with "Our Father who art in heaven" (Matt. 6:9).

The word *Father* indicates that only children of God can use this prayer. How, then, do we get into God's family? Through faith in Christ. John 1:12 states that only those who have received Jesus by believing in his name have the right to call themselves children of God.

I've noticed that some Christians pray to the heavenly Father in his own name. They conclude their petitions by saying, ". . . in your name, amen." But that's like saying, "God, I don't need Jesus to usher me into your presence. I come on your authority, not his." That's a mistake, for God has not invited us to approach him without a mediator. We should no more pray in the Father's name than say the Father or the Holy Spirit died on the cross. Jews attempt to pray to God directly, but because they fail to approach him through Christ, the one mediator God has appointed, the prayers of the Jews are ineffective.

Don't commit the same mistake. Perhaps you've been praying in the Father's name unintentionally. But that doesn't make it right. Our only access to the throne of grace is through the Lord Jesus. Only through faith in him are we en route to heaven. So apart from him we cannot say, "Our Father who art in heaven."

Begin with God, Not Yourself

The first half of this model prayer focuses on the Father's glory, not our goals. It speaks of "Thy name . . . Thy kingdom . . . Thy will" (Matt. 6:9, 10).

We tend to think of prayer as a technique by which we use God to fulfill our plans. But Jesus is saying it's more of a means by which we prepare to accomplish the heavenly Father's will. A man who purchased a rare painting asked the famous artist James Whistler for advice on hanging it. "How can I keep it from clashing with the pictures I already have on my wall?" he asked. Whistler replied, "First, take everything off your wall. Then begin with your rare painting. And after that, refuse to hang anything that clashes with it."

We've treated God like that painting. We've tried to fit him into our plans, when we should have been conforming ourselves to his. We've asked the Lord to bless our goals, grant our desires, and satisfy our needs, without so much as considering his glory. That kind of prayer starts off with our problems rather than with the Lord.

Do you put God first in your prayers? I often do not. Our prayer lives, if left to themselves, are like a car with its wheels out of alignment. They will always drift off course. That's why we need the direction of Scripture. It gets us back on the road. And here the direction is to begin our prayers with God, not ourselves.

Pray in Concert with Other Believers

I find it fascinating that the singular pronouns *I*, *me*, and *my* are never found in these verses. However, the plurals *we*, *us*, and *our* occur nine times. Count them:

"*Our* Father. . . . Give *us* this day *our* daily bread . . . forgive *us* *our* debts, as *we* also have forgiven *our* debtors. And do not lead *us* into temptation, but deliver *us* from evil."

Someone penned these words, which illustrate my point:

You cannot pray the Lord's Prayer and even once say *I*.
You cannot pray the Lord's Prayer and even once say *my*.

Nor can you pray the Lord's Prayer and not pray for
   another.
And when you ask for daily bread, you must include your
   brother.
For others are included in each and every plea;
From the beginning to the end of it, it does not once say
   me.

A similar piece asks these questions:

What gives this prayer its power?
It ne'er says *mine* but *our*.
Why does it grip me thus?
It ne'er says *me* but *us*.
What may its beauty be?
It ne'er says *I* but *we*.
It humbles me, but why?
It ne'er says *my* but *thy*.

So pray in concert with other believers. When you're
praying in a group, don't say, "Lord, *I* pray . . . *I* ask . . . *I*
thank you." That turns prayer partners into mere listeners.
Instead, lead them in prayer by saying, "*We* pray . . . *we* ask
. . . *we* thank you." The same holds true if you're praying in
front of a congregation of worshipers. Singular pronouns
don't fit. Use the plurals and let it be the others' prayer, too.

This passage of Scripture is placed in the context of private prayer. Three verses earlier Jesus told us to retreat
into our inner rooms and speak to the Father in secret. Yet
the prayer he gave us has no singular pronouns. In my
private conversations with God, I've found tremendous
fulfillment in saying we, us, and our. I like to think of
myself as one brother in a worldwide family of believers.
Using the plurals is a good way to muster the full strength
of the body of Christ and to avoid selfishness.

Pray with a Zeal for God's Glory

The first petition is made up of four pregnant words: "Hallowed be Thy name" (Matt. 6:9).

The *Good News Bible* translates it thus: "May your holy name be honored." This is a request that our heavenly Father will receive the glory he richly deserves. It's a passionate plea that more and more people will honor him as their God.

Notice the mention of God's "name." Names in the Bible are full of meaning. *Abraham* means "father of a multitude," because the Lord promised to give him countless descendants. *Jacob* means "schemer," and that's just what he was throughout most of his life. *Samuel* means "heard by God." His mother gave him that name because his birth was the answer to her prayers. In the Book of First Samuel we meet a man named Nabal, which is the Hebrew word for "fool." And even Nabal's wife admitted that he wasn't called that for nothing. She said, "As his name is, so is he" (1 Sam. 25:25).

The personal name of God is Jehovah, or more correctly, *Yahweh*. It occurs over six thousand times in the Old Testament. Exodus 3:14 says it means "I am." On eight occasions Jesus himself said, "I am." It sounds like an unfinished sentence. "I am . . . "what? But to put a word at the end of that sentence would limit God. There are innumerable terms that must be placed there. We could say the name *Yahweh* means "I am everything you need."

Do you need strength? He is your strength. As Paul said in Philippians 4:13, "I can do all things through Him who strengthens me." Do you require wisdom? "Christ Jesus . . . became to us wisdom from God" (1 Cor. 1:30). Is it peace you're looking for? "He Himself is our peace" (Eph. 2:14). Perhaps for years you've resented someone who has harmed you, and the bitterness has been devouring you from the inside out. You want to love this person, but you don't know how. "God is love" (1 John 4:8, 16), so let Christ do the loving through you. Whatever your need might be, the Lord Jesus can meet it. He's the great "I AM."

Hence, when we pray, "Hallowed be Thy name," we are saying, "May more and more people trust you for who you are. May they discover your greatness and all-sufficiency. May they allow you to show yourself as the great 'I AM,' and so glorify all that your name means." That's how Jesus wants us to pray.

Pray with a Surrendered Will

In the opening of Matthew 6:10 Jesus teaches us to ask, "Thy kingdom come."

Every kingdom has a king. And since it speaks of "Thy kingdom," God himself is the king, and we are his subjects. This is more than a request for the literal kingdom that Christ will set up at his second coming. It's a plea that our Lord will rule and reign in people's hearts *now*. I'm sure you've prayed, "Thy kingdom come" many times. But have you surrendered yourself to the Lord? Is Jesus your king? Are you his servant?

The Navigators are a group of Christians who emphasize discipleship. A businessman once asked Lorne Sanny, then president of the Navigators, how he could know when he possessed a servant attitude. Sanny replied, "By how you act when you are treated like one."

The idea of a kingdom is foreign to us in America. We're part of a democracy—a rule by the people. We're our own kings. But when we come to Christ, everything changes. We take our place as servants before the king of the universe. And that requires a surrendered will.

The next petition sheds a different light on the same truth: "Thy will be done, on earth as it is in heaven" (Matt. 6:10).

Human nature is so inflated with self-will that when we finally say, "Thy will be done," we're like a tire that runs over a nail and becomes deflated. The pressure is now gone, and we can be healed by Christ. Even Jesus, as he contemplated his death on the cross, prayed, "Not My will, but Thine be done" (Luke 22:42).

A teenaged boy and girl once approached Lehman Strauss and asked how they could know the Lord's will for their lives. He replied, "If God told you his will, would you obey him instantly?" The girl said, "That all depends." And the boy answered, "How can I say yes, if I don't know what it is?" They were unwilling to yield themselves to God until they could compare his ideas with their own. And thus their hearts were still opposed to the Lord, unsurrendered.

Scripture outlines the will of God. It says that he is "not willing that any should perish but that all should come to repentance" (2 Peter 3:9 NKJV). *Thy will be done.* First Thessalonians 4:3 declares, "This is the will of God, your sanctification; that is, that you abstain from sexual immorality." *Thy will be done.* The Bible commands us, "In everything give thanks; for this is God's will for you in Christ Jesus" (1 Thess. 5:18). *Thy will be done.*

Can you pray like that? Do those texts express the desire of your heart? In heaven our Lord's will is done joyfully, promptly, and without any murmuring. It's fulfilled with a surrendered heart. That's what we need if we're going to follow Christ's guidelines in prayer.

Pray in Total Dependence on God

In Matthew 6:11 our Lord's Prayer tells us to petition, "Give us this day our daily bread."

While having lunch with a man years ago, I offered to say thanks to God for the food before we ate. He was quick to express his offense at the idea. "I work hard every day," he complained. "The only person I have to thank for the food is myself. God had nothing to do with my eating this meal."

That man failed to see that his daily health, strength, and mental capacity were gifts from God. It never occurred to him that he could have a heart attack, stroke, or an accident that would leave him paralyzed and unable to work. He didn't think he was dependent on God, but he was.

Jesus told us to say, "Our Father." Just as a child trusts his father to put food on the table every day, we should look to God to supply all our physical needs. The word *bread* here means that we can expect our heavenly Father to grant only our needs, not our greeds. If we are praying for luxuries, we have become addicted to them, and that's the opposite of dependence on the Lord.

Pray with a Repentant Heart

Next, Jesus told us to pray, "And forgive us our debts, as we also have forgiven our debtors" (Matt. 6:12).

At first glance this might look as if we earn God's forgiveness and thus our salvation by forgiving others. But there are three reasons why that cannot be. First, Ephesians 1:7 says, "We have . . . the forgiveness of our trespasses, according to the riches of His grace." That rules out any idea of merit. Second, our verse does not say, "Forgive us our debts, *because* we also have forgiven our debtors." And third, we saw in the word *Father* that this is a prayer for people who are already children of God. Their salvation, therefore, has already been signed, sealed, and delivered in heaven.

What, then, does this petition mean? Jesus wants us to show God an attitude of repentance. But merely asking for pardon doesn't prove we've repented. A criminal on death row might beg to be spared, yet not feel sorry for the murder he committed. Repentance implies a brokenness of heart. And the best way to prove that is by forgiving others. An unforgiving spirit is a form of pride, and pride will always block the path of repentance.

Some time ago I was counseling a mother whose daughter had been killed by a drunk driver. She possessed an unquenchable passion to see the drunk driver punished. Her purse was stuffed with letters she had written to radio and television stations, newspaper editors, lawyers, and judges, crying out for justice. I asked her if she was a Christian, and she said yes. So I went on, "Are you willing to forgive the man who killed your daughter?" She stared at me through breathless seconds, then shook her head from left to right. The woman had said, "Forgive us our debts, as we forgive our debtors" many times. But she stood self-condemned by her unwillingness to forgive.

Who needs your forgiveness today? Perhaps your own spouse or some other family member. Fill in this blank: "Father, forgive me, as I also forgive _____." That's tough, isn't it? Repentance is not easy. But God looks for it in our prayers.

Pray with a Holy Dread of Sin

In the opening of Matthew 6:13 Jesus tells us to say, "And do not lead us into temptation."

The same Greek word, here translated "temptation," is used in James 1:2, which tells us to consider it all joy when we encounter various "trials." There is no contradiction between those two verses. Our Lord uses trials and

temptations to strengthen our faith. But we can never hear
this word *temptation* without being reminded of our vul-
nerability to sin.

Think of your greatest temptation. It might be the
desire to overeat, gamble, lust, cheat, steal, or swear. Does
the thought of that enticement to sin cause you to shiver
in fear, or to rejoice? Can you honestly pray, "Lord, don't
let me encounter that problem today"? If you can, you're
living with a holy dread of sin, just as Jesus wants you to.

Pray with a Warfare Mentality

The prayer, "Deliver us from evil" (Matt. 6:13), can be
translated "Deliver us from the evil one," namely, Satan.
Many versions of the Bible render it that way. Are you
aware that as a Christian you're in the midst of a spiritual
warfare? Do you believe in a personal devil? The earlier
words "Thy kingdom come" remind us that there is a rival
kingdom at war with God's. Its ruler is competing with the
heavenly Father for our souls.

When a Christian decides to divorce his or her spouse
because the two of them have grown apart, the problem
runs deeper than a conflict of personalities. Satan is driving his wedge between them. On the two sides of the
abortion debate are the pro-life and pro-choice advocates.
But behind them stand the Lord of heaven and the prince
of darkness. When a nonbeliever tells you he's not interested in trusting Christ, it doesn't mean he's not cut out to
be a Christian. It means Satan has blinded his eyes. And
when we believers grow indifferent to the Great
Commission, which tells us to make disciples of all people, we can be sure Satan has lulled us to sleep.

There's an invisible war waging in the universe, and
you're in the thick of it. Prayer is no cute little ritual. It's a

wrestling in the strength of God's Spirit with principalities and powers. Never forget that prayer is war.

Worship God in Prayer

The prayer Jesus gave us concludes with these words: ["For Thine is the kingdom, and the power, and the glory, forever. Amen"] (Matt. 6:13).

There are no requests there. Just worship. This takes place apart from our asking God for something; we just tell him how wonderful he is. Here's an example from a hymn:

> Jesus, the very thought of Thee
> With sweetness fills my breast;
> But sweeter far Thy face to see
> And in Thy presence rest.
>
> No voice can sing, no heart can frame,
> Nor can the memory find
> A sweeter sound than Thy blest name,
> O Savior of mankind.
>
> O hope of every contrite heart,
> O joy of all the meek,
> To those who fall, how kind Thou art;
> How good to those who seek!
>
> Latin hymn 11th Cent.
> Translated by Edward Caswall, 1849

Do you ever pray like that? I don't mean poetically but worshipfully. Other hymns that illustrate worship are "How Great Thou Art" and "Great Is Thy Faithfulness." They are full of loving tributes to God. Worship is the supreme purpose for which we were created. Weave it into the fabric of your prayers, and it will make a dynamic difference in your life.

Personal Application

There you have the Lord's Prayer. Just five verses in the Bible. A mere sixty-eight words. You can recite it in less than a half minute. Yet it takes a lifetime to practice its principles. It instructs us in everything we need to know to become prayer warriors in our own right. It leaves us without excuse if we are inept at prayer.

At the beginning of this study I said that we need not apologize for calling this the *Lord's* prayer. But let's not stop there. Let's make it *our* prayer, too.